What Do You Want to Do When You Grow Up?

"A remarkable, on-the-mark book for anyone twenty-five to eighty-five who is planning a job change or contemplating retirement." — Norine G. Johnson, Ph.D., president, American Psychological Association

"*What Do You Want to Do When You Grow Up?* is extremely helpful in a practical way as it reminds individuals that financial security and physical health are important, but to make sure that personal fulfillment is not ignored. Though advertised for retirees, wannabe-retirees, or midlife job swappers, this book should be required reading for high school and college students because the steps and exercises help the reader focus on personal goals. Dorothy Cantor and Andrea Thompson have written a winner that provides useful guidance in an easy-to-follow and -read book that assists the individual 'starting the next chapter of your life.'" — Harriet Klausner, *Midwest Book Review*

"Jimmy and I have always believed that whenever one door closes, another opens. *What Do You Want to Do When You Grow Up?* is a book for anyone who is retiring from the workforce and is seeking a new direction for finding personal fulfillment. Dorothy Cantor shows you the way to take stock of your life and map out plans for a future that will be meaningful and deeply satisfying — with perhaps the kind of excitement and enthusiasm you felt as a child, just starting out on your grand adventure." — Rosalynn Carter, former First Lady and author of *Helping Yourself Help Others* and *Helping Someone with Mental Illness*

What Do You Want to Do When You Grow Up?

Starting the Next Chapter of Your Life

Dorothy Cantor, Psy. D.

with Andrea Thompson

Little, Brown and Company
BOSTON   NEW YORK   LONDON

Originally published in hardcover by Little, Brown, January 2001
First paperback edition, January 2002

For information on Time Warner Trade Publishing's online publishing
program, visit www.ipublish.com.

Library of Congress Cataloging-in-Publication Data
Cantor, Dorothy W.
    What do you want to do when you grow up? : starting the next chap-
ter of your life / by Dorothy Cantor with Andrea Thompson. — 1st ed.
        p. cm.
    ISBN 0-316-12714-0 (hc)/0-316-12798-1 (pb)
    1. Retirement.   2. Career changes.   3. Self-actualization
    (Psychology).   I. Thompson, Andrea.   II. Title.
    HQ1062.C37 2001
    646.7 — dc21   00-037081

10   9   8   7   6   5   4   3   2   1

Q-MART

Designed by Meryl Sussman Levavi/Digitext

Printed in the United States of America

To Gerry,
with whom I want to do whatever
I do when I grow up.

CONTENTS

ACKNOWLEDGMENTS

Without the participation and help of a number of significant people, this book would not have been possible. My gratitude to them all:

First, to the many people who generously opened the stories of their lives to me and allowed me to share them with others. Gracious guinea pigs, they were willing to discuss the highlights of their career paths and interior journeys, including some pipe dreams, regrets, and the occasional woeful misstep. Specifics of their stories have been changed in order to ensure their privacy.

To the myriad patients I have seen over the years, who continue to teach me about human development and who inspired me to look into the question of how to achieve well-being later in life.

To Barbara Cantor, my administrative assistant, for taking on the thankless task of transcribing hours of interviews, and to Jim Racine, my research assistant, for saving me from having to do the literature searches myself.

To Marcy Posner, my agent at the William Morris Agency, who loved this project from the beginning and shepherded it to a home at Little, Brown. To Bill Phillips, my editor there, who recognized its value from the first time he saw the proposal and used its lessons to fashion his retirement. To Deborah Baker, who nurtured the book to completion, and to the creative people at Little, Brown who ensured its success.

And, most important, to Andrea Thompson, who did the writing, for being such a pleasure to work with and for hearing my ideas and my voice and having the talent to so exquisitely translate them into language to which readers can relate.

What Do You Want to Do When You Grow Up?

Starting the Next Chapter
of Your Life

CHAPTER 1

THE CAPACITY TO GROW, THE NEED TO CHOOSE:
An Introduction

ince you have bought this book, or at least picked it up to thumb through in the bookstore, clearly the question posed in the title has piqued your interest. Perhaps it reminded you of a similar question you were asked every now and then by one of the adults in your life when you were a kid — "What do you want to *be* when you grow up?"

Now you're the adult, you have *been* the teacher, designer, lawyer, accountant — and now the question of what *to do* next is beginning to sound increasingly salient.

Maybe lately the job feels less secure or less satisfying than it used to, you are experiencing an uncomfortable sense of your own dispensability or a dispirited sense of ennui, and you're starting to think you need to reboot your life in some way.

Maybe now, with the bulk of your working years behind you, you're wondering if you were ever in the right job to begin with and whether you might try a stab in another direction.

Or maybe you did what you set out to do in your career, you made your big bucks, and you're stalled now by an abundance of possibilities and a dearth of vision.

Or you're about to retire, a lot of the old people you know seem to be idling the days away, and you're thinking you want to make sure that doesn't happen to you.

As a psychologist with a private practice consisting primarily of people in their early forties to mid-sixties and beyond, I can tell you that you have much company. Many, many of the men and women I see in my practice these days are asking themselves, What next? That's something, I believe, that their parents and grandparents didn't stew about, and something that has much to do with particular aspects of the extraordinary, even unique times we are living in.

Listen to these two conversations I had recently:

From her first position as an assistant to her current one as administrative director, Carla P. has been engaged in the start-up and growth of a now twenty-year-old series of learning materials for the parents of developmentally disabled children and the teachers who help them. She loves what she does. She will soon be leaving what she does, because, she said, "It's a whole new ballgame. For funding reasons, they need someone with a degree and credentials I don't have. Also, they probably should have a younger person now, fresh ideas."

She's not unhappy about moving on, she's ready for something new, but she is having trouble getting over the feeling of "being put out to pasture." Carla is fifty-nine. "In looks, I think I can *pass* for forty-nine," she said with a laugh. "And I *feel* like thirty-nine."

She has a few plans — extended visits with friends in Europe and with her married daughter in Seattle, taking adult education courses — but Carla was frowning as she described them. "I wonder if that's just about filling time," she said, "and I've got a lot of time left! Besides, working with these kids and families has just been a huge, huge chunk of my life — not just in hours but emotionally, mentally." She talked about her father, "a mechanical engineer with the phone company who worked there from age twenty-four to age sixty-five, one day after his birthday. The line of demarcation between work and after work was sharp; he never talked about the job again. In fact, he never talked about it while he was *in* it." She didn't see such a sharp line for herself.

Another scene: A large gathering of friends and family, three generations' worth, come together to celebrate a youngster's second birthday. Sitting around on the back porch after the cake had been eaten and the presents opened, several of us listened as Sam J., a self-described workaholic, talked about the imminent sale of his business — a hazardous-waste disposal plant that he had designed, operated, and seen flourish — to a major national manufacturing facility. It was a sale, said Sam, that he felt was necessary and inevitable, for several reasons, and that would make him a millionaire several times over. "We'll be set for life," he said. "I can hang it all up."

"What will you do then?" I asked him. "What comes next?"

A long pause. "What next? I have absolutely no idea," he said. "I can't imagine not doing this work. I'm terrified."

Sam, the father of the birthday boy, is thirty-eight.

In their experiences and thoughts, Carla and Sam illustrate some of the parameters of our dramatically changed world of work, indeed of our lives:

◆ There are many years ahead.

Carla is right — in all likelihood, as statistics show, she's got a lot of time left. A fifty-year-old woman today, barring heart disease and cancer, can expect to hit age ninety-two. What to do with those after-working years becomes more critical when remarkable increases in longevity and general health offer us a substantial amount of potentially productive time.

◆ Retirement isn't what it used to be.

For some individuals, retirement still retains its traditional shape, as it was for Carla's father — leaving the workforce at a particular age, sometimes after an extended period of service in one company, marked by cleaning out the desk and a farewell luncheon with the boss and coworkers. But for many other men and women today, that picture no longer applies.

For one thing, an increasing number of people, we are learning, fully intend to keep in the job world indefinitely. For several reasons, not the least of them pleasure in the effort, something like 80 percent of baby boomers say they plan to continue working after "official" retirement age. According to some predictions, 7 million people age sixty-five and older will be in the labor force twenty years from now. "Our new life patterns," says a report from the Wellesley Centers for Women, "may render retirement all but obsolete." (And that suggests, the report goes on, "we should be trying to plan a future that includes both work and time for family and play, continued growth for ourselves. . . . We must consider our psychological and social well-being, which . . . are widely discounted and underappreciated in Western society. An awareness of the options life offers in later years may enable an individual to exercise choice, which is essential to emotional health.")[1]

◆ What we do as work, to a significant degree, defines who we are.

Carla, too, has not so much a job, as her father did, but a career, work that engages "a huge chunk" of her time, her emotions, and her thoughts. Her career shapes not only her days and weeks but her identity and sense of fitting in with a big picture. Sam, too, "can't imagine" not doing the work in which he's invested himself.

For many of us, work constitutes a large part of how we are regarded by the world and how we regard ourselves. The anticipation of nonwork, then, makes retirement a far more frightening and complicated matter than imagining the simple relaxation it meant for a previous generation.

◆ Careers are no longer etched in stone.

Sam is part of a growing cohort of relatively young individuals who are startled by the realization that the future just might be an open book. Our affluent, prosperous society enables many people to "hang it up" fairly early on in life, even at the tender age of thirty-eight.

In addition, the fading of the paternalistic company —

don't do anything too wrong and you won't get fired, stick it out for forty years and you'll be granted a pleasant if not lavish pension and stopgap medical insurance until you die — has many workers exploring options, hiring themselves out as independent contractors, or switching to entirely new tracks along the way. Indeed, some studies indicate that young people now starting out in their work lives will have four or five different careers, not just jobs in the same field, before they're through.

So, *What Do You Want to Do When You Grow Up?* is a book about changes and transitions relating to your personal world of work, a book about what you will be doing in that period of life when you'll be spending less time than you are now at the work you do now.

It may be a period that includes the chance to do or be what you want to do or be, for the first time, and one in which you will experience the greatest freedom you've ever had. Perhaps few expectations will weigh on you, in the smallest and the largest ways. All of which sounds grand, except . . . the wide openness of it can be scary! If you have had little exposure to so many degrees of freedom, making choices is daunting.

Still, you may not be entirely convinced that thinking about some answers to the question in my title is really necessary. Some protests you may be making (and why I'd like to talk you out of them):

◆ "I'm sixty, too old to start thinking about all this."

Not so. Sixty isn't old anymore. The percentage of Americans that age or older has more than tripled since the beginning of the century. My profession, in fact, continues to adjust the concept of what constitutes an "older adult," now identifying subgroups as "younger old," "older old," and "oldest old" — that last being over eighty-five, the category that's increasing faster than any other age group.

In addition, you in your later, later years may not be what you now think you will be. Researchers in one nationwide survey asked a number of adults how they envisioned themselves twenty or thirty years down the road. What did they expect that time to be like? What did they imagine they'd do more and less of? What would they lose? And the results showed that many people have skewed notions of what *really* goes on with older folks. A fair number replied they thought they'd probably be unable to drive a car, they'd get a serious illness and have trouble walking, become dependent on their kids. Wrong. Only a small percentage of old people actually have such experiences.

You have vitality to look forward to. Your eighty-year-old self may do just fine in terms of the physical and cognitive strengths necessary to a satisfying life, so at sixty you're certainly far too young to start viewing yourself as on the shelf. (In fact, had you been born into certain Native American tribes, you would not even have been considered an "adult" before age fifty-one.)

♦ "I'm forty-five, too young to start thinking about all this."

You should start thinking about all this, even in your energetic and busy forties. It is not too early to make good plans and ready yourself. For one thing, you may need time — a good bit of it — to explore, experiment, and learn. Alan J., for example, an accountant, always dreamed of his first love, farming, and in his early forties began what he called "a slow, slow journey in that direction." Today, fifteen years from the start, he says he feels "like a kid in a candy store, building fences, caring for animals, mowing, fertilizing, liming pastures" on his seventy-acre farm in southern New Jersey. As was true for Alan, getting where you want to be won't necessarily happen overnight.

But for another thing, like my friend Sam, you may anticipate major career-course changes in your future, well before you finally hang up your hat.

So you're not too young to start pondering these matters. You know it's unwise to wait until you're sixty-five to do some financial planning or physical shaping up. Neither should you postpone giving attention to your psychological well-being.

◆ "Well, once I'm not working such long hours, I'll just enjoy life — so what's to figure out?"

Nothing, if you know what you want to do, and if what you want to do will truly engage you. For seven years before he sold his practice, a psychologist collected in a shoebox under his office desk little pieces of paper, on each of which he had written down an area he wanted to explore someday. Today he is involved in all but one. He's learning to run a television station, volunteering at a local community college studio to pick up the basics of camera work, sound work, directing, and editing — everything but machine repair ("I am intentionally avoiding that one," he said). He conducts a dog obedience class once a week and trains horses, one of his youthful enthusiasms. Keeping his hand in his profession, he serves as an unpaid mental health technician at the Red Cross. He teaches a course on safe-driving techniques for the elderly and plays bass fiddle in a bluegrass band. About learning to speak Spanish, the one pursuit he hasn't yet begun, he said, "*That* can wait until I can't get around anymore."

He figured it out, carried it through, and is immensely satisfied with the life after the job he is continuing to fashion for himself. For many more individuals, and perhaps for you, the visions are less clear — enjoying life, doing everything you want to do, will somehow "happen," as long as you have your health and some money in the bank.

Media messages have fostered that attitude. They promise us all will be well as long as, first, we keep healthy — "Life's an adventure because you're over fifty and still exploring" (and you're taking your vitamins and "natural" laxatives) . . . read this book about the latest cancer-fighting/heart-disease-fighting diet . . . buy this video on yoga for seniors. Second, find a good investment adviser — "Anything you can dream of doing later, you should begin building now." Eat right, walk two miles a day, have enough money to live reasonably well. The rest will take care of itself. Get ready to go out and do all those things you've always wanted to do. Life after the job will be the dream of a lifetime.

Not necessarily. Many people who have entered the after-the-job stage of their lives find themselves asking if there isn't supposed to be *more to it*. More meaning, purpose, or excitement, perhaps. More of the deeply refreshing sense of "This is where and what and who I want to be." I know, because many such people come to my office for counseling.

There was Frances B., an office manager for a midsize construction firm, who spent the first year after retirement fixated on an array of aches, pains, and trips to doctors (until she figured out what she wanted to do with the rest of her life and just as suddenly felt better).

There was Paul H., who elected to retire early, bought the property next door to his suburban home, and installed a swimming pool and tennis courts. Relishing his new-found freedom initially, he soon found that being able to indulge his love of sports every day seemed frivolous.

There was Alex W., an investment counselor who cut back his business to one or two clients and a few hours a week, who said he was waking up in the morning feeling aimless and vaguely unsettled and was looking at the clock each evening, deciding if it was late enough to go to bed.

Like Frances, Paul, and Alex, the individuals who have shared their thoughts with me for this book are accomplished, intelligent people who, in general, have put a sensible amount of thought and effort into getting ready for life after work. During our conversations, I asked each of those men and women two questions: When did you begin to take steps to ensure your good health into the future? When did you begin financial planning for your later years? And interestingly, every one of them could give me chapter and verse on those scores — fifteen years ago they quit smoking and started exercising, ten years ago they taught themselves something about investments; they get yearly checkups, they meet with financial counselors. These were the same men and women, some of them, who hadn't planned in any way what they were going to *do* with their healthy bodies and comfortable bank accounts.

They hadn't given attention to how to spend their time in the ways that would please their hearts and minds and psyches, to discerning the pathways and the pursuits that would keep them growing.

And many of them are not as satisfied as they expected to be. They're not sick, they're living where they want to be living, they have things to do and friends to meet — but they sense they're keeping busy, not genuinely moving on. Life feels a little flat. They're asking themselves: What next? Is this a chance to come into my own, finally? How do I do that? And for some: Have I done enough? Will I leave a mark?

Surprising? Certainly this doesn't quite jibe with that media image of the fifty-plus crowd as uniformly vibrant, full of beans, no doubts. A distinguished group of journalists, psychologists, and researchers, gathered to discuss emerging issues for Americans fifty and older, concluded that newspapers, magazines, and TV do not adequately and accurately take note of the huge and growing population of older Americans — "unless they're tap dancing or bungee jumping."

A fifty-seven-year-old communications executive was persuaded by an attractive benefits package to take early retirement, a story I have heard from a fair number of the individuals I have interviewed for this book. Although if he had his druthers, he'd still be working, the decision to leave was his own to make and he doesn't regret it, one year later. Still: "I was not psychologically prepared. One day you wake up and you don't have a job to go to. The questions come. You think, Whoa, somebody has decided I'm no longer productive. Or, I can't or don't contribute to the success of an organization any longer. Or even, Gee, I'm too old to work. It can be traumatic."

So, yes, I'd guess that if you're like most people, you might benefit enormously from taking this opportunity to figure out what you want to do next, and what "enjoying life" really means to you.

One more voice of protest you may be raising about now:

◆ "What's this about 'growing up'? If I'm not grown up by this time . . ."

Here is what I would call the great and reassuring gift that has emerged from research in the field of developmental psychology in recent years: growing up keeps on going. Each life is a work in progress, change is possible, and growth is essential at any point within it. In fact, human-needs theory proposes "growth" — the compulsion to be creative and productive — as one of the three basic necessities of an individual's life, along with "existential" needs, or the material and physiological things required to survive, and "reference" needs, or the need to be with other people.

Growing up can and should be a continuous, dynamic process across the life span, and we know a lot about what makes the process successful.

This book is about that process, about uncovering the pathways and pursuits that will be meaningful to you, for reasons you may not fully perceive right now.

◆ ◆ ◆

Can you make the transition to after work or to a really new kind of work in a thoughtful, orderly, and satisfactory way, not with fear and trembling but with confidence that what you are doping out for yourself will be rewarding, invigorating, and fun? Absolutely, if you put some time and energy into charting a path.

Can life after work be richly fulfilling, intensely satisfying, marked even by a newfound, delightful, astonishing resiliency and buoyancy of self? Definitely, if you know what you need and how you'll get it.

That's what this book will teach you. *What Do You Want to Do When You Grow Up?* is not going to talk the usual talk about preparing for the second half of life — start early to invest wisely, keep your bones strong with weight training and calcium supplements, learn to manage your HMO. You know that already. Neither will it offer the typical self-help book's paste-on solutions, the literary equivalent of the psychiatric hospital's occupational therapy — ways to keep occupied rather than to develop a genuine occupation, which is the pursuit of activity because of an inherent, personal meaning, need, or calling. We're all bombarded these days with paste-on solutions, too: take classes, go bird-watching, meditate.

What we *are* going to talk about can be summed up as the capacity to grow and the need to choose. I will show you how to configure new plans based on some sound psychology and on a clear-eyed awareness of the past — the combination of influences, innate and external, and experiences that constitute your life so far, the private drama in which you are the star. We will look at what went before, in order to find some clues for the future.

By the time we are finished here, you may be thinking long and hard about an old fork in the road you didn't take. You may decide to let some genies out of the bottle, rekindle old dreams, go back to a critical juncture and make something turn out better than it did before. And you may be realizing to your delight that such a move is well within the realm of possibility.

Maybe you'll find yourself focusing on hidden or long-forgotten passions and talents that can be uncovered and that might guide you in a new direction.

You may begin to change certain assumptions about yourself and to explore a path you never thought of before but sense will supply an element that has been missing in your life and that you crave. You will decide this is your time to "discard the old, embrace the new, and run head-long down an immutable course," in the words of Jacques Cousteau.

Or maybe you'll want to do more of what you've always done, but in a different way.

In the process, you may rediscover what it is to feel and think with the enthusiasm, wonder, and freshness of a child, when all things seemed possible. And now you can temper that childlike approach with the wisdom and experience of your years in the world, which have taught you useful lessons about your personal strengths and weaknesses, likes and dislikes.

What Do You Want to Do When You Grow Up? outlines a personal journal or an autobiography, one you will construct for yourself.

I'm going to ask you to think about three broad phases: your childhood and adolescence, your main working years as an adult, and midlife, where you may be right now. These have been your first three chapters or acts, so to speak, the broad stages that will have included certain universals or developmental tasks. Within each, you will take a look at how it all played out for *you* — what you wished for, what you did, and how you did it.

What did you start and stop? What got in your way? Whom did you admire? What tickled your fancy?

Did you have a family label — the good student or the clown or the little actress?

Did you finish your education with a clear idea of what to do next?

How did you get your first job? Has your work life involved change? Was it change you sought or one you had foisted upon you? What's the last new thing you learned?

Did you always play it safe? Do you regret that now?

You will explore a number of such questions, to which there will be no "right" or "wrong" responses. My job is not to impose solutions and "shoulds" (and you will find none of them here) but rather to pose suggestions that will help you tease out those clues and see the patterns they form. There's no threat. No one else need know about any of this. Take your time, make it a leisurely excursion, and have some fun with it all.

When you've finished reconstructing your story, you will have many pieces of information about yourself, including a keen sense of how much along the way you chose and how much was dictated by societal models, others' expectations, or necessary circumstance. From them, we will begin to develop your individual road map into the future.

I'll show you how to pull those pieces together to sketch a plan for this next part of your life — the time in which there will be few rules, the time in which the choices will all be up to you. We will play something of a Twenty Questions game, looking at what I called the ten motivators and the ten activators in your makeup. Your motivators and activators will point you in some directions, and they'll indicate what it makes sense for you to do next and how you'll go about doing it.

Along the way you will hear from many individuals who talked to me at length over the past months about their lives and next steps. In particular, we'll be following eight men and women who generously and in detail shared their histories. Some have already officially retired, some are still working. A few surprised themselves by finishing their autobiographical excursions in very different places than they had first anticipated. So may you.

◆ ◆ ◆

Centuries ago, when the world was still largely unknown, cartographers sometimes wrote at the edges of their maps, in those spaces indicating lands or seas still to be discovered, the words "Beyond this place, there be dragons!" The prospect of exploring the unknown is usually daunting, and sometimes scary. But the dragons go away — indeed, turn out never to have been there — once the map is drawn. Only by drawing your map, and charting the uncharted, can you design a life of your own choosing.

I don't know what you should do when you grow up. But from my training, practice, and research, I *do* know what it takes to keep growing and to tap the deepest sources of satisfaction. And I do know how to lead you through an exploration of your past and your present that may suggest dynamic possibilities for your future. By the end of this book, you may not know exactly what the rest of your life is going to be like. But you *will* know this: what themes or leitmotivs have been threading through the years; how much of your identity has been defined by your work, and what would be a smart thing to do about that; what you need in order to promote and sustain the exhilarating feeling of keeping on growing.

What you should do with the rest of your life — to keep growing, to be fully alive — is as personal as a fingerprint. There is no one right way. Just don't leave the future to chance; do not assume that after you stop working, all will fall comfortably into place. When you and I have finished here, you will possess a measure of new awareness that will enable you to make good choices and take action, to design the years ahead, not wait for them to happen. In any case, you will come away with the powerful conviction that you have within you, as do we all, the gift for endless self-renewal.

CHAPTER 2

RETIREMENT DREAMS, JOB REALITIES

I invite you now to think a bit more concretely than you probably have done so far about your retirement, still to come or already past, and about your job, the one you've left or are working at right now.

Equip yourself with a pen or pencil and a blank yellow pad, or better yet, a spiral-bound notebook. We begin here what will by the end of our exploration amount to a brief autobiography. This very personal, for-your-eyes-only diary will constitute a road map through significant aspects of your past and present, with a few trails plotted out into the future.

At the top of the first page, write:

WHAT I WILL BE DOING WHEN I AM
NO LONGER SPENDING MOST OF MY TIME
AT THE WORK I AM DOING NOW

We might call this inventory "My Life after Retirement," but, as mentioned, it may be most useful and provocative to interpret in the broadest terms that word *retirement,* which still conjures up for many of us a concrete image of a particular age and an abrupt transition from work to nonwork — an image that no longer matches the reality of many American adults. Possibly it has no particular resonance for you, as it does not for the editorial director of a large publishing house, who said: "I don't know how to spell the word *retirement.* My attitude is, I keep running. And somewhere in the dark there's a cliff. And I don't want to see it before I fall off." If you don't want to see the cliff, and plan to be found dead at your desk at age ninety-seven with your mouse still in your hand, "What I Will Be Doing When I Am No Longer Spending Most of My Time at the Work I Am Doing Now" is the more apt heading.

Some of your first impressions may concern the deliciousness of sitting at an outdoor café late on a Monday morning, enjoying a leisurely latte and the day's paper, of taking in a movie on a Wednesday afternoon, and so on. Those adventures are lovely to contemplate and may indeed become real pleasures in your future, but let yourself sink deeper into the fantasy as well. We want this to be not a once-over-lightly glance but the considered anticipation of a major portion of your life. Ignore any practicalities or impossibilities that come to mind; don't worry here about

what you'll be able to afford or whether you'll need to sub-
let the apartment or what your children will think about
what you intend to be up to. The idea is to let your imag-
ination drift and come up with the best visions. As you're
drifting and envisioning, make notes.

Some people who explored their retirement dreams
with me found themselves continuing to focus on established enthusiasms, as was the case for Thomas H., a mechanical engineer with a major international corporation:
"I've always had a lot going on besides my job and
family — plants, hiking, fooling around with computers,
music. These have been pretty intense hobbies, and I'd plan
to get even more intense about them. I'll build a green-
house out back, for one thing, really get into my bonsai in
a major way." Others imagined entirely new paths: Emma
C., a department store buyer, dreamed of moving to Siena,
restoring an old house, and keeping bees. Still others
thought in terms of filling in old gaps or making up for
perceived past lacks — spending more time with the family, doing good works for others in order to "give back."

If you have already officially retired, or at least segued
into a downsized work mode in your life, make your notes
on how the days have been passing. Consider whether
what you anticipated for this time has matched the reality
you have entered.

To give you some inspiration before you begin or some
comparative company after you finish, meet now four men
and four women who sketched their journeys for me. In
the chapters to come, you'll get to know them well. Their
thoughts are noted as they talked them over with me in a
series of lengthy one-on-one interviews. Record your own

thoughts in whatever manner comes most naturally — a shorthand list may do the trick, or you may be inspired to write out a mini-essay on your after-the-job dreams and present-day realities.

Regarding life after retirement, or what they thought they'd like to do when they are no longer doing what they are doing now, here's what our eight friends had to say:

JACK G., AGE 58
school guidance counselor
still working

Jack has been at work since age seven, when he ran a paper route, and he's hardly stopped since. "As kids, my brothers and I had to sneak in the playtime," he remembered. "Maybe half an hour of stickball in the evening, or I'd ride my bike for an extra fifteen minutes after the papers were delivered."

He's made a career in a Wisconsin school system, with enough years in to consider retiring, although there's no pressure on him to do so at this point. He has given some thought to when that time should come, but not too much thought to what he'll be doing when it does. He does know, he said, that "when you're not working, it can be a hell of a long day. I get a two-and-a-half-month summer vacation, and I can tell you, that is not always as great as it sounds."

Jack's list went like this:

"I won't have to commute, which is getting to be a bigger headache every day. No traffic hassles.

"Plus there'll be nobody telling me what to do. I can do whatever I want."

That's all Jack said. Looking ahead, he liked the idea of fewer hassles and less responsibility but suggested only the vague "I can do whatever I want" to take their place. Probably because Jack is a man who hasn't enjoyed many opportunities to dream since he was a little boy, he found it difficult and unfamiliar to let go and fantasize. After some urging, Jack went back to the drawing board and tried to be a bit more expansive and creative.

Take two:

"I'll go fishing. Read Louis L'Amour novels. Maybe take a place in Florida for a month every now and then.

"Doesn't sound like much! When I was a kid, I wanted to be a baseball player. Maybe I could coach kids.

"I want to travel some. I've never been out of the United States. Or even to a lot of parts of this country.

"I used to like to collect stamps. Haven't done that since I was about ten. I probably still have my old albums around. Lots of stamps since I stopped collecting.

"I'm good with my hands. There's a lot of stuff to do around the house. I see myself replacing the fence, building a deck out back."

That was better.

ISABELLA R., AGE 45
communications director for a medical
equipment manufacturer
still working

Divorced, with no children, Isabella lives in a condo in Connecticut, a short drive from her job and near almost all the members of her large family. Although she's far from contemplating retirement, Isabella thought our assignment was great fun and at once saw some pleasing possibilities: "I will never again have to wear panty hose, little silk shirts, little boring blazer suits, and little heels. And I never will!" She had some more serious ideas as well.

Isabella's dream:

"I used to say when I was in my twenties that if I wasn't married by forty, I'd pack up my mom and me and move us to a slightly seedy town on the shore, and we'd live on the cheap like beach bums — 'under the boardwalk, down by the sea!' That still seems like an excellent idea.

"Because I've always been happiest by the ocean, I'd have a summerhouse at the beach, a drip-dry house, a place you hose down every so often. No fuss. This reflects, I think, my growing urge to simplify my surroundings. Eliminate things.

"In the winters I'd rent an apartment somewhere in the Caribbean or the Keys, get a job crewing on a boat that takes people out to go snorkeling, and bring my mom down every so often and cook us fish dinners every night. It seems, at least, I will have three places of residence!

"I'll take regular retreats. In fact, I keep cutting out articles about retreat houses, and the ones that appeal to me are places where you stay in a little cell-like room, join the community twice a day for morning meditations and evening meals, and spend the rest of the time on your own.

"Study art restoration? A possibility. I actually had this thought for about fifteen minutes when I was in college, but somebody told me I'd have to take chemistry, and that turned me off. But the thing about the *idea* of art restoration is that it sounds wonderful to me to work for hours, in a solitary place, with tiny brushes and tools on a square inch of some old painting, bringing it back to life.

"My own work life has been almost entirely verbal and mental, and while I think I am exceptionally good at producing annual reports on company earnings and press releases on defibrillators, I want to employ my artistic and manual skills, which are also good, although essentially unused and totally unrecognized by the world. And I think, too, a beautifully restored painting is a more significant achievement than a beautifully produced annual report."

MAX L., AGE 58
vice president with a food company
still working

Max didn't need to be sold on the idea behind this book. "Three things I know," he said. "First, I am so far from grown-up, it's a joke. Second, decision time is coming up for me in a few years, and I feel either pulled in seventeen directions at once or no pull at all toward anything. And third, nothing I am doing at the moment logically suggests what I should be doing next."

Life after the job, his own next act, has been so much on his mind that Max has recently been putting together a cartoon and joke book, "a kind of 'you know you're over the hill when . . .' Not that I actually feel over the hill. It's the thing about still growing up."

His dream:

"Write my memoirs. So who wants to read Max's memoirs? Nobody I can think of, and that includes my wife and two kids. But I've been making notes for the past couple of years, my musings. I want to see if there's a sense to all the stuff I've been through, which has been a lot.

"Dance. It always surprises people that for a short, kind of pudgy guy, I'm a better-than-average ballroom dancer. So I want to do more dancing. Maybe take lessons.

"Maybe get back to comedy somehow. I was never actually *in* comedy, in a professional sense, but I was the kid king of the one-liners."

SHEILA H., AGE 55
senior partner in a law firm
still working

Sheila raced through college and law school and has been a working lawyer since age twenty-four, taking six-week maternity leaves when each of her three children was born. In private practice for the past twelve years, she's been handling mostly employment law. Although her successful negotiations of cases involving age and sex discrimination make her feel she's "doing good," Sheila said, "I am not enamored of the law."

She looked ahead with difficulty, her visions for life after the job consisting mainly of possibilities considered and then rejected:

"My retirement dream — I have none. My present goals — I have none.

"I think the most successful retirees are those who are

really eager to leave their jobs because they want to do something they absolutely love but could pursue only after hours because they needed to make a buck. And I'm not talking about the golfers. That may be fun, but that can't be the whole life. There must be a passion.

"I want to find a passion, but I'm not sure where to look. I once had a social passion, to change the world, but that's gone. I still feel it intellectually, but not on the gut level.

"I've always been interested in literature, art, music. I could sign up for courses, but the idea of sitting through classes now is appalling to me.

"Exercise and read books, which is what both my husband and I do now in our spare time. But we don't do much of anything else, and reading and working out hardly seems like a life.

"Community activities don't interest me greatly. I do not like working with groups on boards. It bores me. I did those things from time to time because I thought I should.

"Volunteering. I've done a fair amount of that, too, and generally I have not been terribly comfortable with it. For example, I always helped with the holiday fairs in my kids' schools, found myself running a booth, setting up the bagels and the cakes and all, and I just felt silly. I'd think, Why am I doing this?

"So, my retirement dream — I want to start thinking about it, but I feel paralyzed because I can't come up with anything that sounds truly appealing. My best skills are legal skills, and I think that after I stop working, that's what I want to get away from, do something completely different. But what, I don't know."

BARRY J., AGE 66
electronics manufacturer
retired twelve years, turned investor, consultant,
and arts critic

Barry "gave myself the gold watch," as he puts it, at age fifty-four, retiring as head of an electronics firm in Pennsylvania. Before "officially" quitting work, he had given the matter a good deal of thought: "I was motivated by two things. First, by what I saw as a need to lower the level of stress in my life, because the business I was in was doing bad things to my blood pressure. Second, by my need for security, meaning to have enough income that I didn't have to worry a whole lot about money." Describing his "my life after retirement" plan, Barry remembered back to that time and how it came about:

"This is funny. One of the things I used to dream about was that when I retired, I'd be able to sleep late. And in the first year, I'd do that, sleep until maybe nine or nine-thirty. Now I'm up at six-thirty because I want to get the Standard and Poor's futures. Now that I don't have to get up early, I like getting up early. So that was a dream that came and went fast.

"When I was still thinking about it, I went through a process of trying to understand what retirement meant. I thought about the days, and for me it was never a matter of 'Okay, I'll do the gym on Monday and tennis Tuesday and I'll hang out on Wednesday.' That sounded like going from something to zilch.

"We had an organizational psychologist who was on retainer, kind of cruising around talking to people. I called him in and said, 'I want to retire; what does that mean?' And this guy actually helped me think it through. I realized that in my life I always do best when I have something to go to mentally.

"I'm an antsy guy. I always want a couple of projects stacked up in front of me. So when I left, I had three projects in mind that involved mental concentration. First, I wanted to expand my writing. I'd been doing reviews of performance arts — jazz, dance, some musical theater — for a couple of small papers in our area for years. Decided I'd right away see how I could make that more of a full-time, serious thing. Second, I wanted to learn what a computer was. I knew how to *use* one for a lot of the work I did, but I didn't know what the computer was, so that was on my list. The third thing was, I was going to be a crossword puzzle writer.

"So I prepared to go out. One of these things I actually did, the other two not. Because then other stuff came up."

THERESA I., AGE 58
management supervisor in an oil company
retired one year

Leaving a job she loved, and a company she'd worked for since age eighteen, wasn't Theresa's idea. "I was in a pretty high management position, coordinating various employee aspects of the business, and I would have been happy to keep going for another ten years anyway."

When her firm elected to eliminate that level of management across the board, Theresa was offered a retirement package she couldn't refuse: "If I hadn't accepted it and had chosen to stay on in another position, which I could have done, I was going to end up with a pension that was far less." So, with about three months' notice, she was gone.

She had no big ideas about what she would do when she didn't go to the job anymore, but Theresa believed, at the outset, that keeping busy wouldn't pose any problems:

"At first, I had a wonderful sense that now I could just do whatever I wanted. Because I never had that before in my life. I always needed to be so disciplined, every minute accounted for. I had to take care of a lot of the housework and cooking when I was a kid, plus go to school. My time was never my own. So that was a dream, just doing whatever I wanted.

"Then I figured working on the house my husband and I had just bought in New Jersey was going to be my new 'job.' I threw myself into that, stripping miles of wallpaper, painting, caulking the old windows. And this took me six months. And then that was the end of that.

"I do some gardening.

"I've always liked cooking, and I do fancier kinds of dishes now.

"I'm thinking of doing some kind of volunteer work.

"This maybe sounds odd, but I do a lot of window shopping. I don't like to stay home. I'm an excellent bargain shopper and I get all my Christmas stuff done six months early."

One morning Theresa was sitting at her kitchen table having coffee, "and I was looking out the window seeing people going off to business. They've got their attaché cases, you know, and I just wanted to grab mine and go with them." Her experience over this past year prompts her, she said, to offer some advice: "I'd say to anybody who's working, in their forties or fifties or sixties, stick with it as long as you possibly can. Unless you're really ready to quit, don't do it. Don't think you're going to sit home and enjoy it, because you won't. You're so accustomed to that business atmosphere, so accustomed to getting up and dressed and out in the morning, talking to people all day, even if it's a confrontation or a difference of opinion. You're on that bus, and then all of a sudden the bus stops and you get off. What then?

"I haven't figured it out for myself. In general right now, I'm kind of taking one day at a time."

DAVE W., AGE 64
talent agent
retired two years

Dave had hoped to leave a business he never particularly loved fairly early on, but "I didn't get enough money together, so the plan I'd had to quit working when I hit fifty wasn't a practical reality." When he did finally, at age 62, sell his share of the agency to his partners, Dave embarked on what he anticipated would be the best of times in his suburban California town.

He said now, "If you want me to talk about retirement visions or life-after-the-job dreams, I can give you a very specific before and after picture. Here goes.

"First, the money issue. I always thought my wife and I would do some fabulous things, travel around the world. I'd do a lot of sailing. I'd go hiking. Many, many active, travel-oriented fantasies. But when I did finally quit the business, I had enough money for us to live okay, but not so much that I didn't have to make some hard choices. So some of those fantasies had to go, mainly that kind of traveling.

"This was a blow, but not a terrible one, because I still didn't see how I would have enough time for all the things that interested me. I had a vision that there would be plenty to keep me occupied in the world — a vision of a very civilized, urbane, relaxed sort of leisurely life, with me a very civilized, relaxed sort of person. These were the images:

"Spend whole days reading books. Also, I'd go to lots of museums, bookstores, take daylong, unplotted walks through the city.

"Take better care of myself — more bicycling, playing tennis, going to the gym.

"Do some good work volunteering.

"Take up some interest in my neglected spiritual life.

"Pursue my hobbies, especially playing the piano and writing music.

"Spend some great times with the grandchildren.

"Now, the reality, the after picture. The first, immediately reality was — liberation! I started bicycling around town, never took the car. Took long walks. Played with the kids. Joined a bunch of organizations. Did all sorts of things. Six months into retirement, I suddenly found myself in a violent depression. I got some therapy, which I am still in.

"So, I'm starting to get a little handle on all this, including that a lot of those visions are just not coming about. For example, if I've spent two days over the past two years reading books, that's a lot. I think I actually read *less* now than before. The 'good works' volunteering I have not done, although I made some sporadic attempts in that direction and realized they were basically gestures, unsatisfying.

"Attention to my spiritual life — I had a couple of study sessions with the rabbi, read from the Torah a couple of times, sort of let that all drop. Those organizations I slapped myself into, the meetings — a lot of this has turned sour, lots of politics involved, so I've dropped several.

"So what do I do? I sleep a little later. I go to the gym, infrequently. The grandchildren are a joy. And here's a surprise — I spend a lot of time at my desk. I used to say to my father, who's retired in Florida, 'Why aren't you out fishing or golfing?' And he'd say, 'Well, I have paperwork.' 'Do it tomorrow,' I'd say, and he'd say, 'No, no, I have all this paperwork to do.' Now I'm saying the same thing. And I wonder, Why am I always at my desk? What's with all the paperwork?

"So regarding my retirement dreams and plans, I would say I thought I was prepared, and I turned out to be misprepared."

MAY Y., AGE 84
psychologist in private practice
still working

After sixty years in school testing, running clinics, and seeing private patients, along with three years as an Army

WAC during World War II, May claims she's cut back on her psychology practice in New York, although "I will sometimes see ten or twelve patients in a day, not much fewer than it used to be." She is a widow, mother of four, and grandmother of ten.

May gave some thought to this request for retirement dreams, "but it's not a matter that's much on my mind usually," she said. "I haven't figured out how long I plan to keep working, because why should I? The work is great.

"So if I stopped, one thing I might do — although I doubt I ever will — is move up permanently to the little cottage we have upstate, which we used as a vacation place. I love it, but what the hell would I do up there all the time? Just sit on the top of the hill.

"I'd go to the museum more, because I always miss the exhibits I want to see.

"I'm a photography nut. I have shoeboxes full of my photos that could be organized, and that would take a lifetime.

"Go to some places. I always wanted to get to China, to see the gorges and Yangtze before it gets covered over.

"So that's about all that occurs to me."

◆ ◆ ◆

Your second assignment: settle down on your couch with the beverage of your choice and your notebook and pencil. Turn to the next sheet and write at the top:

My Job Realities — Fifteen Good Things (Besides Money) I Get from My Job

If fifteen don't occur to you, try to come up with eight or nine anyway. These we might call the positive payoffs of what you do for most of your day.

Here's a fact to give you pause. For the past twenty or thirty or however many years, about two-thirds of your nonsleeping hours have been wrapped up with the job, going to and from and doing the work. In fact, according to some studies, over the past two decades you probably have gradually been working longer — three to four additional hours a week, or about four extra weeks a year at the job!

Later, in Chapters 4 and 5, we put your personal world of work under the microscope, because looking at the job and all those hours you've spent at it from some possibly new angles — such as how you have handled changes along the way or made decisions or accepted compromises — just may provide significant clues to what you're going to do next and how you'll get there. Right now, consider a "fifteen good things" inventory.

Remember that many people — like Jack — tend to think of the job and then life after the job in terms of unpleasant matters they do now that they won't have to do or deal with then: work twelve-hour days, coexist with a difficult boss, fight rush hour, and so on. And it sounds delightful *not* to have to do all that. Such images and anticipations can also amount to a psychologically sound defense mechanism, in a sense, against the transition from work to nonwork that looms in the future, a transition

36

that's always going to be unsettling to some degree. It's not at all unusual for individuals to focus on the hassles they'll be leaving behind, in other words, as a way of beginning to separate emotionally and mentally from the jobs they know they won't have anymore.

But now contemplate the flip side of the picture. List your positive payoffs in the ways that have meaning to you:

I like heading out the door in the morning looking clean and spiffy.

I get a lot of satisfaction from showing the young people around the office how the business works.

My in-laws know I have a big job and think I'm hot stuff.

Delight in my home, since I'm out of it so much.

That nice time of getting back together with my partner in the evening.

Weekends . . . a business card . . . a reassuring hierarchy.

Give these items some thought. A fair number of them, you may realize, profoundly influence the shape of your days and your feelings about the life you're living. Perhaps a few of them also constitute significant aspects of your identity. These are the job features that involve what psychologists describe as one of the three aspects or factors of "work meaning" — in addition to a financial aspect (you get paid) and a social aspect (you interact with other people), work provides a significant psychological payoff, or a self-image.

A lawyer who is giving some serious attention to the matter of what he wants to do when he grows up, when his working life is behind him, told this story about an associate: "He was a good lawyer, a very neat and decent and capable man. In his mid-fifties, well off, he decided to get out. Almost immediately he realized that he missed the work, but not just the aspect of *going to* work every day. Being a lawyer was the significant element of his identity.

"So after about a year in this terrible depression, he went back and asked for part-time status — 'just to keep my hand in the game,' he said. They hired him back, but in the state he was in, he couldn't do the work well, couldn't reengage. When his probation period was up, he wasn't renewed. It destroyed him."

Think about the self-image you get from your job. Within the first few minutes of meeting someone new, don't you inevitably "explain" yourself as a stockbroker, an optometrist, a computer programmer? Perhaps for you, as for most of us, your job is not just what you do. To a powerful degree, it is what you *are,* how you live publicly and creatively in the world.

Which suggests, of course, that the end of your job or official working life may come as more of a jolt than you now anticipate.

Our eight friends talked about their job realities and positive payoffs:

JACK, 58
school guidance counselor

"Someplace to go.

"People to talk to.

"If I'm working, I'm being good. I never act like a dope when I'm working. Plus, as I've said, I never didn't work.

"I'm good at what I do.

"There's no one home all day anyway, because the kids are out on their own and my wife works.

"I feel important.

"Sometimes I've really been able to help someone, help straighten out a good kid who's been heading down a bad path. I've made a difference. Some of these kids look at me like I'm a big shot. That's a positive payoff, my being a big shot to somebody.

"The work isn't really that hard, so I get a sense of being productive without busting my tail.

"The hours aren't bad. This is a nine-to-four gig, and I like that.

"Some good friends on the job, some of them for years.

"There's a fair amount of variety in the course of the day."

ISABELLA, 45
*communications director for a medical
equipment manufacturer*

"I spent a lot of years commuting into Manhattan, and now I just jump in my car and get to work in fifteen minutes, against traffic, and maybe it sounds simpleminded, but I love the freedom of coming and going in my car.

"This place has an on-site gym and a walking track outside with exercise stations, and I've gotten into working out since I've been here.

"Great cafeteria. This changed my eating habits entirely, from skipping lunch and having a big dinner, to a healthful lunch and a light meal at night. Lost some weight, which was nice.

"I do a lot of work with printers and suppliers, and I like the fact that I meet different kinds of people, not all white collars.

"My boss gives me a lot of latitude. That makes me feel admired, trusted, and appreciated.

"Nice people, mostly.

"There are a couple of opportunities for moving up. I don't know if I *want* them, but they're there, and that makes me feel good."

MAX, 58
vice president with a food company

"I feel respected, which I guess I need since on the home front, like Rodney Dangerfield, I don't get no respect! At least, sometimes it feels that way.

"Mental plus physical involvement. At the end of a day sometimes, I fall into bed completely bushed, and that's a great feeling. I'm on the road a lot, out at the plants, and I like that aspect of being on the move.

"At certain points in the past, the job was the one part of life that was going okay. I could go to my office, focus completely on what I needed to get done that day, and do it, and feel good. Everything else was in various states of chaos. Maybe you'd say the job kept my mind off my problems.

"The food business is actually kind of interesting. It

came as a surprise to me, but I've got a good business head, a good head for figures and details. Once I settled down and sort of gave in to what I was doing, it was satisfying.

"Before he died a couple of years ago, my father — who most of my life basically wrote me off as a schmuck who wasn't going to amount to much — saw me become a success in this business, saw me get the promotion to vice president. So that was a payoff that came from the job."

SHEILA, 55
senior partner in a law firm

"Status.

"Intellectual stimulation. Not all of the time, but at least a lot of the time. Although that hasn't been so true in the past few years, because I've been essentially coasting along at something I can do with my eyes closed. I seem to get bored if I do one thing for too long, and I've been doing one thing for too long now.

"Improving my brain, when I have to learn something new, or at least holding the fort against further deterioration.

"Something to get me up and out in the morning, or else I tend to inertia.

"Interaction with other people. This is critical to me. During a stretch in my career I was doing primarily research and writing, and the extreme isolation was anathema to me. I felt bored and restless. I need that interaction with other people.

"Occasionally, a real sense that I've accomplished something positive and helped people."

BARRY, 66
investor, consultant, arts critic, retired manufacturer

"Small privileges that make life easier. That organizational psychologist I talked to said, 'You better get used to lots of little things about your job that you're not going to have when you retire or you're working on your own. Right now, you want to send something to one of your kids, you bring it to your assistant to ship — done. No more. You need to mail something, you're going to have to drag your ass to the post office. You're just an ordinary person with a few bucks in your pocket.' He was right about all that. So there was a sort of level of daily life that was taken care of for me.

"An ability to compete. I love to compete. I love to outperform. Outperforming, in fact, is really more important to me than competing. It's the opportunity to be better than others. So the job gave me the chance to measure up against others, and be better.

"Power, in the sense of recognition. This is something I figured out from my talks with the psychologist. He said, 'You're going to lose a lot of the power you've enjoyed.' I thought about that, what position power had in my set of needs, or whatever you'd call it. I thought first of power as control, and I don't need control. But power is also recognition, and I do need recognition.

"From the writing, the performing arts criticism, I get status and prestige. No sense of power, because I report to an ignoramus of an editor. But I'm well known as a commentator and critic of modern dance, jazz, and musical theater in the New England area, asked to lecture sometimes.

"From the money managing I've been doing as a consultant the past few years, I get humility. You could be right three days in a row, and the fourth day you're completely wrong. Because the world changed. So every day you start with almost a clean slate. I like having to be humble once in a while, so I don't forget who I really am."

THERESA, 58
retired management supervisor in an oil company

"I got insight into people, I'd see what made them tick.

"I got a lot of support. There was really a family sort of feeling. For example, once when my mother was between jobs and money was very tight for us, I asked for an advance on my next paycheck. The office manager asked me why, and I said I needed it to pay the rent. And he wrote out a personal check and told me to pay him back when I could. I always felt people were looking out for each other. You could count on those people the way you could count on friends.

"Levity. Camaraderie. We'd play little jokes on each other, like putting a rubber snake in somebody's briefcase or handbag. Just silly things, lots of laughs.

"I got the opportunity to listen and learn.

"I always had the feeling I was appreciated. I got a number of really nice notes from our vice president — you know, good evaluations, 'another job well done by Theresa.' I kept all those notes. There's nothing like getting a lot of compliments from the upper echelon.

"I'd have to say that in my life, I was most comfortable with who I am, the person I am, when I was in my last position at the company. I felt as though I had power. I did have power."

DAVE, 64
retired talent agent

"A community of people who, in many cases, I cared for deeply and who became close friends.

"But here's the two real positive payoffs, what I got from my job and that I don't have now — feedback and structure.

"On the job, I had somebody saying all the time, 'Dave, I need you to do this . . . you've done this . . . thank you for doing this.' Now, nobody's saying, 'Nice, Dave,' or even, 'Thanks, Dave,' or, 'Dave, get back to me right away on this.' I used to make four hundred phone calls a day, and four hundred people were listening to me and feeding back to me. Being in a service business, which a talent agency is, I had people needing me to take care of large aspects of their lives. I am mostly happy *not* to be taking care of people's lives anymore, but at the same time, all that daily feedback is gone.

"Second, structure. For example, when I worked, I got up early every morning, went biking for an hour or sometimes went to the gym, came home, showered, played the piano for an hour, got all this done and myself to the office by ten. When I stopped working, I couldn't sustain those things for some reason. I'd get into my sweats and sneakers, then I'd think, Maybe I'll go to the gym later, or I'll bike tomorrow. Or I'd sit down at the piano, then get up and say, I can do this later.

"Without the imposed structure, I found it hard to organize myself, or even to hold on to the same values for things. There seemed to be suddenly a lot of self-questioning: Is this how I really want to spend my time? Do I genuinely care about this? Instead of playing the piano, maybe I should be reading a book. Instead of reading a book, maybe I should go to the museum or take the grandchildren out for ice cream. Thrown on my own resources, everything became a decision, and maybe I was making bad decisions. In business, there wasn't time to make bad decisions."

MAY, 84
psychologist in private practice

"My work gives me a lot of gratification. Voyeuristic gratification. I'm as nosy as they come. The more I know about people, the more I want to know.

"It gratifies me also because I'm essentially passive and I like to listen, so it's the perfect kind of job for me. I don't always have to talk. In fact, I rarely have to talk.

"It's ego flattering. People want to look upon me as a minor savior, and that's a role I enjoy playing.

"Diversity, different kinds of people. Wonderful colleagues.

"Opportunities for wider exposure, like attending professional meetings.

"And it does a lot for the grandchildren. My grandchildren think I'm an important lady."

◆ ◆ ◆

Put away for now your "what I'm going to do" and "good things about the job" lists. Of course, feel free to add to or revise them at any point along the way, if you wish. When we're finished, we'll return to Jack, Isabella, Max, Sheila, Barry, Theresa, Dave, and May, and to your own retirement dreams and job realities, for another, possibly revisionist look.

CHAPTER 3

WELL-BEING AND THE AMERICAN ADULT: What Is It? Who Has It?

B efore we plunge into the nitty-gritty of your autobiography, we'll detour through a brief overview of the professional understanding of human well-being.

Family, friends, good food, fine wine, may all be part of the picture, of course, as well as freedom from acute financial worries. But our focus in this brief Psychology 101 is on some less tangible or less easily identifiable elements, specifically the psychological processes that contribute to individuals' sense over time that they're living the lives they should be living.

The Good Life, Well Lived

Numerous surveys, dating way back, have sought to determine what it is that makes older people feel good about themselves or sustain feelings of subjective well-being. Traditionally, such studies have tended to be based on a simple notion: well-being or wellness in later life can be measured, first, by the absence of sickness or "not wellness" and, second, by the assertions of individuals as to how "happy" or "satisfied" they are with their lot ("on a scale of 1 to 5, check off . . .").

Certainly, that's an acceptable starting point from which to draw some conclusions about the well-lived life. Most people do assume that good health equals well-being; and increasingly in this day and age, they recognize that "health" embraces both the physical — a fit, pain-free, and disease-free body — and the psychological — a relative lack of depression, stress, anxiety, obsessiveness, or other elements of discontent. (In fact, the scales of common perception may have tipped lately toward the power of the psychological. A busy internist said, "I have trouble persuading people that there are bacteria anymore. My patients say, 'I have this ailment, it must be stress, send me to a therapist.'")

But traditional methods of defining well-being are a bit *too* simple, we are concluding, and much recent research has aimed to fine-tune the concept of what constitutes well-being in older age. Being "not sick" and, simultaneously, reporting feeling "satisfied" do not quite seem to fill the bill. Neither do overall composites of several measurable factors — income, religion, age, education, gender, and marital status, for example — reliably account for a great deal of variety in individual experiences. While being well educated, financially comfortable, and married, for example, increases the likelihood that one is going to feel good about things in general, not every wealthy Ph.D. with a wife is a contented man.

We need to probe a bit deeper, it seems, to come up with a truly detailed, rich, and textured picture of well-being in the later years, the fulfilled life, or the successfully still-growing person.

To get at that picture, much recent thinking aims at combining and synthesizing the theories and approaches of developmental psychology, clinical psychology, and the study of mental health. Many compelling contributions in these areas originated from individuals whose names are familiar.

For example, Carl Jung, best known perhaps for his writings on symbols and archetypes, may have been the first to put forth the idea of a midlife crisis, which he saw as a radical transition from impulsiveness and instinctual behavior, to acceptance that one is a young thing no longer, and to the consequent gaining of new understanding and self-awareness. Erik Erikson years ago outlined his now well-known "eight ages of man," each one presenting particular tasks to be accomplished. The tasks of late life he defined as "generativity" and "integrity," the failure to achieve which led to "disgust" and "despair" and "stagnation."[2]

Erikson, Jung, and others had different perspectives and terminology. Some of their ideas, as well, have been adapted or occasionally found insupportable by the passage of time and the interpretations of a new generation of social scientists reacting to changing cultural norms and demographics. Nevertheless, these theorists essentially were circling around and coming up with variations on a small handful of fundamental conclusions about just what must be present to enable the older adult to feel good about himself or herself. In her study "Psychological Well-Being in Adult Life," psychologist Carol D. Ryff, director of the Institute on Aging at the University of Wisconsin, consolidates those conclusions into six main features, or core dimensions.[3] Much recent empirical research has been based on these dimensions and has yielded some interesting results — some of which should catch our attention as we consider what you're going to do when you grow up.

So let us picture an imaginary John Smith, a decent fellow who scores high in well-being, and an imaginary Joe Adams, another decent fellow who unfortunately scores low in well-being, and see what accounts for the difference. (An absolute John or Joe as described here does not have a precise counterpart in real life, it should be noted. No walking, talking, live human being is 100 percent all one or the other.)

Six Dimensions of Adult Well-Being

1. Self-Acceptance
John has a positive attitude about himself. He acknowledges and accepts his good and bad qualities; reviewing his past, he deems it, overall, okay.

Joe, however, feels dissatisfied with himself. He is troubled about certain personal qualities, and wishes to be somewhat different than he is. When he looks back, he's disappointed by what he sees.

2. Positive Relations with Other People

John enjoys warm, satisfying, trusting relationships with others. He's empathetic, affectionate, and concerned about the welfare of those around him. Capable of intimacy, he understands the give-and-take of human relationships.

Joe, on the other hand, has few close and trusting relationships. He finds it difficult to be warm, open, and concerned about others and often feels isolated and frustrated. Unwilling to make compromises, he fails to sustain important ties with other people.

3. Autonomy

High-scoring John is a self-determining and independent guy. Evaluating himself and regulating his behavior by personal standards, he's able to resist outside pressures to think and act in ways he finds unacceptable.

Joe is concerned about the expectations and evaluations of other people, relying on their judgments to make important decisions. He conforms to social pressures to think and act in certain ways.

4. Environmental Mastery

John has a sense of competence in managing his world. He controls an array of external activities and makes effective use of opportunities.

Joe has trouble managing his everyday affairs and lacks a sense of control over the external world. Feeling unable to change or improve his surroundings, he's often unaware of opportunities.

5. Purpose in Life

John has goals and a sense of directedness, aims, and objectives for living.

Joe has few goals or aims, lacks a sense of direction and purpose, and perhaps holds no beliefs or outlooks that give his life meaning.

6. Personal Growth

John feels he's continuing to develop. He sees himself as expanding and realizing his potential. He is open to new experiences, he sees improvements in himself and in his behavior over time, or he is changing in ways that reflect greater self-knowledge and effectiveness.

Joe, alas, has scant feelings of improvement or expansion over time. Feeling powerless to develop new attitudes or behaviors, he's bored and restless and uninterested. Joe feels stuck, without knowing why.

John enjoys well-being. Joe doesn't.

In studies of national samples of the population, including young, middle-aged, and older adults, most people at all ages scored fairly well on the first four dimensions of well-being. Self-acceptance and positive relations with others show no significant differences according to age. Environmental mastery and autonomy tend to increase from young adulthood to midlife and then level off.

But on dimensions 5 and 6, purpose in life and personal growth, older individuals tended to come up short. The goals and aims and direction, the openness to new experiences, the sense of realizing potential, were fleeting or unfocused, or for some individuals just not there.

Other studies point to similar conclusions. Significant predictors of psychological and physical well-being in later life, says one, are "life purpose" (zest, fulfillment, contentment), "life control" (freedom to make choices and exercise responsibility), and "future meaning" (determination to make the future gratifying, and positive expectations concerning what comes next).[4]

So many of the men and women who come to me for counseling, and a fair number whom I interviewed for this book, aren't feeling enough of that. Even with things to do, places to go, people to see, a sense of well-being remains elusive.

On the Job, After the Job: Well-Being or Burnout

Vincent J., an executive in the television industry, deciding he had almost more money than he knew what to do with, quit the business and anticipated a pleasant life: "I never planned anything. I thought my wife and I could do all the things we enjoyed but never had much time for because I've been a career-obsessed workaholic for the past thirty-five years. How could there be a problem?"

He knew what he liked — spending time at each of the couple's three homes, in Colorado, Maine, and New York City, and playing with his "boy toys! I love cars, big TVs." And he knew what he didn't like, or thought it would be best to avoid: "I didn't want to get into stuff I knew I was no good at, or where I'd look mediocre. I've always been lousy at golf, tennis, really at all sports, although I'm a great spectator. I'm no good at bridge, basically hate card games."

One and a half years into retirement, Vincent said that "it seems okay," but he confessed to being a little embarrassed: "I'm actually busy as hell on a lot of days, but I feel inefficient. I'm doing a lot of frittering the time away. When I'm not running around, I'm in front of the sports channel." When he gets really restless and bored, he and his wife pull up stakes and go live in another of their homes and socialize with another set of friends for a while.

No longer refueling himself through his workaholic ways, and not yet having figured out some alternatives that would adequately engage and challenge him, Vincent is having a hard time beating back a certain psychological inertia, an understandable reaction to the double-whammy challenge of life after the job — freedom of choice as to how to pass the time, combined with a complete lack of external compulsion to *do* anything in particular. It's easy then to opt for taking himself off the hook, turning to quickly relaxing, passive activities like watching TV or to "running around," which gives him the sense of keeping busy — all of which was doing little to support the concept he has held of himself throughout adulthood as a competent and accomplished man.

The timing of his experiences and impressions is far from uncommon. In one study of several hundred individuals, researchers describe a kind of life-contentment scale that started high: Men who were six months or less into retirement were optimistic, full of enthusiasm and plans. After about a year to a year and a half, however, things were no longer looking so rosy; letdown set in, "future orientation" diminished. Interestingly, several people who shared their thoughts with me referred to the same time frame in identical, life-or-death terms. "You're gonna die in a year," said one, "if you don't find something good to do with yourself." Not literally die, perhaps, but figuratively, from disenchantment, boredom, and a lack of well-being.[5]

Just starting to acknowledge his dissatisfaction, Vincent is looking at a few deals that might return him to the business world. "I'm hitting burnout on this retirement thing," he said with a little laugh. "I'm getting more stressed-out doing nothing than I ever was on the job." There, he said, he never thought twice about staying in the office until eleven or twelve at night when something had to get done, which was often, or coming in on the weekends just to complete work.

His high tolerance for a sometimes heavy workload had a lot to do with felt allegiance to a company he'd been with all his working life and certainly with the nice hefty paycheck he received. But even more important was his awareness that "the place suited my needs in some powerful ways. When I wanted a change, when I felt I was getting too comfortable and going stale, I moved sideways into a new area. My aim was to keep coming up with a challenge, to go at it intensely until I had it down, to know I was doing good work, and then to bring other people along, help them develop."

Vincent's sense of job satisfaction, he realized, came largely from those feelings of control and self-definition. And those, according to various surveys, are the key elements in workplace well-being for many individuals. Employees who complain that they're overworked, and employers who respond to those complaints by coming up with solutions focused on half-day Fridays during the summer or more coffee breaks, are often missing the point, these studies tell us. When those workers who say they're feeling stressed or have hit burnout because of heavy workloads are questioned more closely about their discontent, they often point to issues that have little to do with long hours.

In their study "Prevention of Burnout: New Perspectives," C. Maslach and J. Goldberg describe job burnout as an essential *mismatch* between the work and the person. The two elements fall out of harmony, or never reach it, when an individual feels little control over the work he or she does or when the job provides insufficient reward: "Prominent among these rewards are external ones such as salary and benefits. But the loss of internal rewards — such as pride in doing something of importance and doing it well — can also be a critical part of this mismatch."

And burnout can also grow out of a conflict in values, a lack of synchrony between what the work demands and what principles and values the worker holds dear. Work, we have come to anticipate (unlike many of our parents and grandparents, for whom any job that provided an adequate income was a good job), should contribute to our sense of self-fulfillment and emotional contentment.

Job burnout, write Maslach and Goldberg, with its feelings of frustration, ineffectiveness, or failure, is "a particularly tragic endpoint for professionals who entered the job with positive expectations [and] enthusiasm."[6]

It's clearly not too much of a stretch to draw a simple parallel between on-the-job and into-retirement experiences. Should we not expect a similar endpoint for the Vincents, who sail into after-the-job years with high hopes, positive expectations, and robust enthusiasm, and watch all that good energy wear away? Burnout threatens if he feels not in charge of his days, if he finds nothing terribly rewarding and prideful to do with his time, if he senses he is not realizing his potential, if he lacks direction and purpose, if the fit is bad.

Vincent was well aware he hadn't uncovered a proper fit. If he didn't return to the business world, he said, he wanted to "find something I can really buckle down to and get into. Do something where you don't even notice the time going by." That was a good idea. Vincent was thinking his way toward some serious leisure.

Purposeful Activity, Serious Leisure, and the Power of Flow

A generally well-documented outlook concerning the best way to live the later years is described by activity theory, which tells us that active adults, by and large, are more content with their lot in life than are inactive adults. The more successful one is at maintaining as many old associations and occupations as possible, or finding substitutions for those that are no longer maintainable or desirable, the better one feels.

Seizing the day, in other words, and making of it what you will is more likely to produce a sense of well-being than is sitting around and observing it pass by. But what distinguishes purposeful action from mere keeping busy, or one purposeful activity from another?

A satisfying leisure endeavor, says the Manpower Education Institute, has some of the following qualities:

A beginner can attain a sense of accomplishment.
Basic skills can be mastered readily.
Real proficiency can come with practice.

It has so many facets that it doesn't become tiresome.
It is within your budget.
It enlarges a skill you already possess.
It offers opportunity for self-development.
It provides a change of pace from your routine.
It can be practiced all year long.
It represents a blend of several activities.
It can be pursued in spite of some physical limitations.
It puts you in touch with other people.
It provides challenges to improve or grow or become more proficient in an area of interest.[7]

Find an enterprise or two of that nature, and you serve yourself well, according to the theory of serious leisure, or "the systematic pursuit of an amateur, hobbyist, or volunteer . . . activity that is sufficiently substantial and interesting for the participant to find a career there in the acquisition and expression of its special skills and knowledge." Serious leisure involves "high investment" activities, developed over time, calling for perseverance, an allotment of energy — even, perhaps, "obligation . . . seriousness . . . commitment."[8]

High-investment activities feel so good eventually because they often lead to "flow," identified in his book of that name by psychologist Mihaly Csikszentmihalyi — the delightful feeling of being so thoroughly engrossed in what one is doing that time goes fast or is irrelevant, of being immune to distractions and anxiety, of being centered and focused and in control.

So, joining a fifty-man barbershop chorus or raising, training, and showing champion standard poodles is probably more conducive to well-being in the long run than is spending the same amount of time watching TV sitcoms. But, obviously, if you can't sing or don't like dogs, those activities are not for you. Activities produce sterling pay-offs in direct relation to their personal significance and relevance. High investment, we might say, is in the eye of the investor.

It's safe to conclude that well-being and deep content-ment sink in when at least *part* of how you are occupying yourself involves doing something that produces those "where did the time go?" moments. (And then watching sitcoms or the sports channel afterward, if that's what you want to do, is less likely to feel like frittering the time away.)

What you are going to do when you grow up depends upon who you are. "The self," says one commentator, "is thought to express itself through behaviors and activities, and in turn behaviors and activities actualize, validate and maintain the self."[9] One shoe does not fit all.

Finding the Fit: Four Stories

One of the most delightful memories of her childhood, said Alice S., a former magazine researcher and fact-checker, had to do with afternoons at a bungalow in a Long Island beach town, where she lived each summer with her brother, sister, parents, and grandparents. On the weekends, Alice and her siblings often went surf casting or crabbing with their father, or walked on the boardwalk and played games in the penny arcades. But that wasn't her favorite part, said Alice, now sixty-eight. "The best of it was when I could be completely alone," she said, "which I'd do by climbing up on the roof of our house with a terry-cloth towel and lie there for long stretches, just dreaming away the day."

Throughout her life, looking back, the need to be off on her own was always strong. As a child and teenager in her family's city apartment, she used to set a tiny alarm clock by her bed for six A.M. on Saturday and Sunday mornings, "so I could have that time to myself before the others woke up, creep out to the kitchen and make myself English muffins, have my muffins and milk, and read or sketch." She hardly went on to live the life of an isolate, however. Marriage, three daughters, school volunteer activities, and a job meant that her days were usually "amazingly busy, run by my kids' schedules and lists of things to do. I lived by my lists." During most of that time, she and her husband did a great deal of entertaining and seeing friends, and although she enjoyed the company of others, "I was really never much of a social animal."

Those were all wonderful years, Alice said, not a regret in the world, but that was then and this is now, and now she's created a very different rhythm to her life in the New Hampshire town where she's lived for five years: "I always wanted a small, old house in the country, a house with very few but very interesting furnishings, and that's what I have. I walk into town every morning, chat with some people there, maybe have lunch in the diner, walk home along the lake. I take naps in the afternoon, I listen to music, I read biographies, I sit on my porch and watch the barn swallows and nuthatches through my binoculars. Have a martini or two before dinner, do a lot of e-mailing after dinner." Sometimes she drives up through northern New

England, browsing in shops she passes and perhaps adding an item to her modest collection of American antiques.

Alice's daughters and grandchildren visit often, but never at Christmas, "because I've done enough decorating of Christmas trees in my life," and in the spring she visits or has come to visit one or another of three friends — "my dearest, closest friends now. Three is enough."

◆ ◆ ◆

All his several jobs, said Charles M. — as a printer for a newspaper chain, a production manager for a furniture manufacturer, and a civil servant — were always more of an avocation, the effort necessary to support a family, including seeing four kids through college. His real love was Christian education and service, because "there's been more trouble in the world caused by religion than anything else. Instead of bringing people together, it separates them. And I just developed gradually a very universal idea of what God is all about, and I always felt a real desire to work with youth."

Over the years, from the time he was twenty-two or twenty-three, Charles taught Sunday school, coached kids in basketball, led training workshops and seminars. He quit work-work when he was sixty-two, with the philosophy that "I'm not retiring from, I'm retiring to," and spent the next seven years as a full-time volunteer, often spending as much as ten hours a day helping out in food pantries, coaching kids, or performing some other kind of service. Now, at age seventy-one, he's pulled back from that intense involvement. He wanted time, he said, "to continue my spiritual journey. I'm studying different religions. Just when I think I got the answers, somebody will ask me a question or something will happen, and — bingo — I got to start all over again. So I'm still learning."

But in addition to his spiritual studies, the continuation of a journey that has intrigued him for years, he is expending efforts in a completely different direction: "I have become an excellent house husband," said Charles. "My wife and I talked this out. With her working full-time and me with time on my hands, I could do one of two things. I could either sit around and just sort of eat bonbons, go up to the pool or the fitness center, walk around the track. Or I could clean the house, do the washing and laundry, have dinner ready when she got home, so that on the weekends we'd have time to do stuff together."

He chose to care for the house and be a homemaker, and he's loving it: "You get instant gratification from seeing what you do; seeing a messy house, I clean it and it looks nice and smells nice. Also, I enjoy working in the yard. When we moved here, there was a kind of wilderness area out back, and I've cleaned that up, cut down vines and branches, and put in a beautiful garden." He loses track of the time when he's weeding, planting, watering, he said. "I just love that way of being creative."

It all fits in with what he thinks he's kind of missed all his life, Charles said: "If I were to start all over again, knowing what I know now, I'd try to relax more. Take time to smell the flowers, like they say. Just enjoy the simple, everyday stuff in life, have a greater appreciation of what's around. That's what I'm doing now."

◆　◆　◆

Somewhere in her mid-forties, Julia G. found her life's passion and began an apprenticeship that culminated one year ago in the opening of her own specialized design studio.

"I was always into craft projects," said Julia, now fifty-one, "even as a kid. Then as a grown-up, I had my various phases." While working as a substitute teacher, raising two children, and handling her dentist husband's scheduling and billing, she indulged her love of handcrafts whenever she could manage the time: "I was a big one for taking courses — quilting, furniture stenciling, weaving. I went through a maniacal needlepoint period, when I learned something like thirty-five different stitches — the rya, the diamond eyelet, the Algerian eye stitch, the rice stitch, all this complicated stuff. When the whole family had needle-pointed bedroom slippers, including my parents and all my aunts and cousins, I decided that was enough of that."

Julia had been encouraged to become a teacher. She had hoped to study applied arts in college but capitulated to the wishes of her parents, who worried how she'd earn a living, and majored in education instead. While she enjoyed her students over the years, "my heart was never really in teaching. I was always drawn to the practical or decorative arts, to the visual and tactile elements, although the idea of being a decorator per se never appealed to me. I didn't want to be buying beautiful things for other people, I wanted to be making beautiful things." A museum lecture and workshop series on textile design pointed her to a new path.

"I loved everything about it from the first moment," Julia said. "I couldn't believe how excited I was to begin learning this wonderful, colorful, very ancient and very modern craft. I felt as if I were practically feasting on all the colors and fabrics and paints." She took adult education courses, collected reproductions of swatch and pattern books from old textile firms, and gradually found several artists who were working in the field and were willing to let her observe their techniques: "I practiced every spare moment — block printing, screen printing, making paper impressions, preparing the cloth for printing, developing designs on paper in gouache, the water-soluble paint that looks a lot like textile dyes. I even fooled around with printing photographs on cloth."

Finally, Julia took a leap: "My children were grown, I had a friend who was willing to take a chance along with me, I had a little inheritance money and some added support from my very generous husband. I quit teaching, and I leased a small studio space." There, she and her partner produce one-of-a-kind textiles that a seamstress fashions into decorative pillows, crib quilts, and little girls' dresses, which are sold through several specialty shops in the city. She has also now moved from student to teacher, instructing an occasional novice designer in the basics of working with textiles. "I'm obsessed," Julia said. "I'm at the studio sometimes fourteen hours a day, and the rest of the time I am eating, sleeping, and dreaming about this work."

◆ ◆ ◆

Carl K. opted to retire at age fifty-five from the Midwestern university where he was a professor of English. He'd spent almost his entire teaching career there, beginning twenty-five years earlier, and "liked most of it," he said, "disliked some of it." The least satisfying stretch was his four-year stint as associate dean of the college, "very little teaching and a lot of administration. What you do as an administrator is facilitate other people to do what they're trained to do, and you don't do what you're trained to do." The best of it was supervising graduate students, "coming up with intriguing topics for their research and theses, brainstorming together. I feel really successful in that area, because most of my students have gone on to get really good academic jobs. And now some of my graduate students are having graduate students — my grand-graduate students!"

But Carl has other success stories as well. "My interests have always been sort of all over the map," he said. "One of the first things I did when I got my first job out here as assistant professor, and started making a salary, modest though it was, was build my own harpsichord. I always had a fascination with that instrument." He then found another professor who knew how to play, and arranged a swap — he'd teach her German in exchange for harpsichord lessons.

A published poet himself, Carl was instrumental in securing for the university the collected manuscripts and letters of a well-known American poet. "I got to spend quite a bit of time with him before he died," he said, "which was thrilling." When he became interested in the issue of children's rights, he put together a curriculum of reading material on the subject that has been widely admired and distributed. During two terms as a visiting professor at a university in Argentina, he wrote essays and a novel, never published, centering on the politics of that country and the plight of the "disappeareds." And during his sabbaticals, Carl pursued another love, archaeology, "being a kind of informed observer and water boy on some digs in Central and northern South America."

Two years after leaving his teaching job, Carl is very busy. The informal band of amateur musicians he put together years back is still going strong: "Sometimes we've been down to three people; once we had eight, which was fantastic." He's been to Geneva to attend world human-rights meetings and to Argentina as a guest lecturer at the university. He's trying to launch a poetry quarterly. What's really got him excited lately, he said, "is the possibility of becoming a kind of itinerant teacher, go here and there as a freelance and see where I end up." He's applied to participate in a program his university offers to provide teachers for military personnel on U.S. bases around the world, and has signed up to teach a writing workshop at the small liberal-arts college in Michigan where he was an undergraduate.

"It's all great stuff," Carl said, "the right mix for me, because I always want to be making a positive contribution to the world, and because I always want to keep traveling. Basically, it's all exactly what I should be doing."

◆　◆　◆

Four individuals with four very different ways of experiencing life after the job.

One finds well-being in relative solitude, a retreat from the kind of bustle that characterized her former days, and in living at a pace and in surroundings that call to her soul.

For another, after he thought through a spouse's needs and schedule, the satisfaction is in combining the simple daily pleasures of caring for a house and garden with private study and contemplation of issues that define and animate the human spirit.

One is delighted by singular, "obsessed" absorption in a demanding craft, perfecting particular skills.

Another is happiest on the move, with ten things going on at once, continuing a number of old interests and a rewarding profession, and "doing good."

And yet as different as their lives are, each one said very much the same thing:

"It's a joy to get up in the morning."

"I'm loving my life right now."

"The days fly by."

They quite clearly knew something about flow, those stellar moments.

Each had successfully adopted what I call a creatively aggressive approach to growing up and had figured out a way of life, including daily activities that were personally meaningful and actively chosen, that suited his or her most compelling needs. Each had taken hold. And each enjoyed a strong sense of the agentic self, the self as a man or woman desiring a certain accomplishment or result and capable of producing it.

All of which underlines the real point about serious leisure and high investment, and the connection to well-being. Continuing to grow up means not so much having a lot on your plate but reaching an ever better accommodation between who you are and what you do. When you are free to choose what you will do next, as you are now, and when you make those choices according to internal needs and proclivities, you're on the right path. You will take an action not because you're afraid to try something else or because you can't think of something else, but because the fit is there.

◆ ◆ ◆

Those internal needs and proclivities that will most satisfactorily shape your future have a strong toehold in your past; what went before has a lot to do with the good life, well lived, to come. So it behooves us to take a thoughtful look at the "what went before," the subject of the next several chapters, in which we somewhat arbitrarily divide your life into three broad segments or acts:

Act One: your life from early schooldays up through age twenty-one or so, the point at which you completed your education, and childhood was officially over and done with

Act Two: your working life, from young adulthood and first job, and on up the career ladder

Act Three: what I've called the great plateau, midlife, beginning somewhere about age forty-five or beyond, the place you may be at right now

As you sketch out the salient details of your autobiography so far, you will be painting a portrait that suggests powerful clues for that Act Four still to come — not only your talents, likes, and dislikes but the critical issue of how good you are at setting, attaining, and readjusting goals.

CHAPTER 4

FROM "I'M GOING TO BE AN ASTRONAUT" TO "I'VE GOT TO PICK A MAJOR": Preparing for the "Real World"

lexis W., a hotel and restaurant manager, remembers the first six years of her life as "a dreamy, delicious time. My sister and I played dress-up games for hours on end. Or we'd line up every one of our dolls and stuffed animals on the floor, a hundred of them, and put on shows with them as the audience. I'd lie on my bed studying the flowers in my wallpaper and imagine I was in a fantastic garden with elves."

Then came school, straight into first grade at age five and a half, "in a very small, very strict, very traditional Lutheran school, and midway through the first week, I remember very clearly a feeling of, Whoa, life is getting serious! But I also completely *got* what was expected of me, what I was supposed to do. I was straight A's through eighth grade — a little star. Grammar school was my shining hour."

Schoolwork continued to present few hurdles for Alexis throughout high school and college, but toward the end of that stretch she found herself in "my most addled hour. Put something in front of me and tell me to learn it, no problem. I still knew what I was supposed to *do,* but what I was supposed to *be* threw me for a loop. No one was telling me that one."

Alexis thus neatly summarized the road many of us followed from earliest schooldays to the point at which we were considered, by the world if not always by ourselves, officially educated. It's a passage Erik Erikson describes as proceeding through the developmental tasks he labeled "industry," for the school-age child, and "identity," for the adolescent and emerging young adult.

As a young schoolboy or girl, you realized — maybe with that sense of "whoa!" Alexis talked about — that you now needed to bend your attentions to gaining certain academic and social skills. You learned to apply yourself to the work you were given and you figured out how to get along in a group of other kids pretty much like yourself. You also made a lot of comparisons with those other kids, gaining a sense of your own competence according to how successfully you stacked up against your peers. If all went well, you developed a fairly sturdy idea of yourself as an individual who could handle whatever came to you.

With adolescence and beyond, the years from roughly age twelve to twenty or twenty-one, life became more complex. At first you worked hard to fit in with the crowd; later on you needed to split off from the crowd somewhat to develop a more personal identity. Even as you enjoyed accumulating skills and gaining mastery over many more elements of life, the question was no longer so much "What do I do next?" but "Who am I now?" Struggling with issues of identity involved for the first time trying to bring a number of disparate "selves" — your values, beliefs, talents, enthusiasms — into one coherent whole, the self with which you sailed or lurched into the world of the grown-ups.

Let us now get down on paper a bit about your personal passage from industry to identity, Act One of your autobiography so far. In particular, think about the choices of those years — what they were, and how and why you made them.

◆ ◆ ◆

Begin at the beginning: what did you want to be when you grew up? Perhaps, like some small children, you knew — and announced to everyone — that you would be a policeman, astronaut, or doctor, or maybe a rancher who raised horses. Probably, like most very young children, your thoughts tended to follow specific boy and girl lines: Jimmy plans to become a football player or a fireman; Jenny plans to be a ballerina or an ice skater.

Psychologists describe those earliest dreams as the first stage an individual passes through along the road to an eventual career choice — up to about age ten, the "fantasy" ("I'm going to be an astronaut") holds sway, during which thoughts of future possibilities may have a lot to do with notions of romance or adventure or all-powerful activities, and not too much to do with real possibilities. (Not always, however. Mike M. remembered his boyhood dream: "I wanted to become a shirt manufacturer, because my father was one. All the other kids in the neighborhood wanted to be hockey stars or ballplayers. I intended to grow up to make shirts." In fact, Mike made a career in the retail clothing business. Dorothea L. had "progressive fantasies. First, about age five, I was going to be the owner of a horse and buggy that carried just-married brides and grooms through the park. Then, a waitress, a hairdresser, a Radio City Music Hall Rockette, a piano teacher, the inventor of my own line of beauty products, a ski instructor, and a summer camp director. The last two I actually became.")

After the fantasy, young Jimmy or Jenny enters a "tentative" stage that can last through high school, in which each begins to take note of what he or she probably can and can't do. Gradually, real interests become more important, as does a burgeoning sense of personal capacities and abilities.

Stage three, the "realistic" stage, usually coincides with the college years and plays out in the context of Erikson's identity-defining developmental task. Now comes some coolheaded consideration of parameters and practicalities: I think I'd really enjoy being a forest ranger, but how many ranger jobs are there? Can I afford two years of graduate school to get the necessary degree? Can I make enough money at it? Will I have to move far away from my family, and do I want to do that?

Right now, think back to the beginning, your fantasy stage, and what you longed to be when you grew up. Whether or not you became the astronaut, ballerina, or rancher, of course, is not the point. What may be the point is the glimmer within the fantasy that tells you something about yourself that still holds a suggestion for the rest of your life — you had an adventuresome streak or you loved applause or you were a save-the-world kind of kid.

Recall that fantasy now, and how much of a hold it had on you.

Your next page:

WHAT I FIRST LONGED TO BE WHEN I GREW UP

JACK, 58
school guidance counselor

"I wanted to be a baseball player, major leagues. I loved Mickey Mantle. I listened to all the Yankee games on the radio. When we got TV, I remember I was so excited.

"Like I said, we kids didn't have a lot of fooling-around time, but I played stickball in the street with my friends whenever I could. I used to imagine myself hitting a home run and being cheered by the crowd. Being the batting champ."

ISABELLA, 45
communications director for a medical
equipment manufacturer

"For a long time when I was a kid, I wanted to be a nun and work in a leper colony for children. I didn't even know what a leper colony was, but I read it somewhere. I made a nun's outfit for one of my dolls and had her bandaging up sick dolls. I'd get a couple of my little friends to play school with me, and I was in my glory when I could be the teacher, who of course was a nun. I'd make a habit for myself out of a sheet and have my friends sit in front of me and lead them in singing beautiful songs. I was a wonderfully kind, beneficent, beloved nun teacher.

"There was a period when it seemed most of the girls in my parochial school fell in love with the nuns, everyone jostling to be the one who carried Sister Agnes's bag back to the convent for her and so on. So this I'm-going-to-be-a-nun dream wasn't so unusual at that age, but it was especially intense with me and lasted for quite a while. And it wasn't the spirituality of it that was appealing, but rather this image of caring for these little children."

MAX, 58
vice president with a food company

"From the time I was about five years old, I wanted to be a comedian. I was always making jokes and people were always laughing. Then, in my early teens, that evolved into the idea that I could be a comedy writer. Because people were always saying to me, 'Max, that's so funny, write that down.'"

SHEILA, 55
senior partner in a law firm

"From about age eight or so, I wanted to be a foreign diplomat. I'd travel around the world, be involved in important decisions, have a real impact on world peace. This was a powerful, prevailing dream throughout my youth, which probably had a whole lot to do with all the heated discussions my parents and their equally politically involved friends were always having around our dinner table. Also, as a family we all went to a couple of demonstrations over civil rights issues, and I thought it was so thrilling and important.

"The dream kind of went into abeyance in high school and college, then came back later."

BARRY, 66
investor, consultant, arts critic, retired manufacturer

"I had no dreams as a kid about doing anything, not until I was in high school. My only dreams or plans were about surviving day to day, emotional survival — survive my mother, survive school. I was terrified about going to kindergarten, first grade. Used to throw up every morning, then head out the door. Every time they said you have to do this by next week, I had a fit. Once we had an assignment to make a little cardboard napkin holder, and I was looking at it and crying because I wasn't going to get it done and the teacher was going to kill me.

"So I was a scared kid with no ambitions. Then when I was about thirteen, for some reason I got a Heathkit and built a little amplifier, doing all the soldering and all. And I was just thrilled that I did it. I loved radios and mechanical things then, and I had this idea suddenly that I'd become an electronics expert. Didn't even know what that meant."

THERESA, 58
retired management supervisor in an oil company

"I wanted to become a nurse. My mother pooh-poohed this idea. In fact, she told me outright, 'No, you don't want to be a nurse, Terry, because you'll have to empty bedpans all day.'"

DAVE, 64
retired talent agent

"I wanted to be an actor. My childhood dreams were extremely clear. In fact, I would say that my work history is really largely a sublimation of my childhood dreams. From the time I was a little kid, straight through school and including all of college and a year of drama school, all I ever wanted to do was to be in theater. It was the absolute preoccupation of my heart."

MAY, 84
psychologist in private practice

"I always wanted to do exactly what I ended up doing. From childhood, I wanted to become a psychotherapist, although of course I didn't know what to call it.

"Because of the rather complex dynamics of our family, I was elected to be or appointed myself to be the emotional caretaker. Although my parents were hardworking and responsible and all that, they needed certain kinds of taking care of, and I became a parentified child in some ways. I was always intent on understanding them and their various peculiarities and needs, and then seeing that my brother and I tried to be accommodating."

◆ ◆ ◆

Maybe you had no particular dream career in mind back then. So remember instead what you most loved to do.

Think of three or four things you especially enjoyed — and why.

◆ Did you love your favorite activity because it felt satisfying and empowering to learn something and to observe yourself continuing to amass more information or higher skills?

◆ Did you love it because it enabled you to differentiate yourself from the other kids in your family, stake out a niche that belonged to you alone, and possibly thus garner your share of your parents' approval and attention?

Growing up one of four sisters, said Elizabeth K., a nutritionist, "we each had our distinct territory. My oldest sister was the brain, great in school. The next oldest was the musician, very accomplished at the piano. And my kid sister was sort of the imp, the little clown. So I gravitated toward being the athlete."

Their parents, she thought, encouraged those roles and separate labels "out of kindness, basically, as a way of letting each of us feel outstanding in some area, and not competing against each other. It strikes me now as a little misguided, maybe, because for one thing I never felt I should play the piano — that was Katherine's territory."

Nevertheless, after pursuing several sports, Elizabeth focused on ice skating, took lessons, spent weekend afternoons at the rink, and earned chevrons she proudly sewed on her skate bag as she mastered each level of difficulty: "The reward was twofold. The best was that this was a thing nobody else in the family could do! And after a while, as I became better at it, skating was just a great joy."

◆ Did you love it as a route to peer acceptance and popularity (as did a man who "got seriously into magic tricks as a kid because everybody wanted to invite me to their parties")?

◆ Was it the one thing that you felt really good at?

Frank L., a computer technician in his late forties, remembers a teenaged enthusiasm that, he said, "now feels a little childish. I started out wrestling in junior high, then in my late teens I got into weight lifting. I was crazy about it. I never got rid of my bench — dragged it with me whenever I moved to a new apartment. I still have it, as a matter of fact." He let weights go by the board, he said, when he got married, started working long hours, had kids and little time. "But back then, when I was no great shakes as a student and had no special talents and was kind of a puny kid, it was the one thing that always made me feel great about myself."

◆ Did your passion perhaps constitute a youthful escape route into privacy and independence?

Said Peter R., a geologist who works for the Department of the Interior: "I grew up in what would most kindly be described as an eccentric household. My parents were distracted by their own problems, which included my father's drinking, my mother's martyred unhappiness, and my sister, who was running wild from an early age. I was left almost entirely to my own devices, which was a blessing in disguise, because I spent hours exploring in the fields and woods around where we lived. I had about ten different collections going at any one time — rocks, leaves, plants, insects, nests, cocoons. I built little wire cages and kept praying mantises over the summers."

Peter's collection, he has no doubt, led directly to his eventual career.

On the next page of your autobiography to date, note:

My Obsessions and Reigning Passions

Jack, 58
school guidance counselor

"Baseball was my favorite activity, although I never played after high school — never had time to do sports in college, because when I wasn't in classes or studying, I drove a cab.

"Stamp collecting was a favorite activity. I'd spend time sorting the stamps, pasting them in my album, finding the countries in the atlas. This was sort of 'playing,' but my parents didn't bother me about it. It was okay, I guess, because they thought I was learning something. It got me interested in geography, which I still sort of am today.

"Then, collecting baseball cards. This I really loved. I spent whatever money I had on cards, more than on stamps, and traded with my friends. Had to be a little more surreptitious about that collection, because my parents thought it was frivolous."

ISABELLA, 45
*communications director for a medical
equipment manufacturer*

"Swimming was my favorite thing. From the time I was very little, I was a water rat. We used to rent a summer place at the shore, and I'd be in the water until I turned blue and my teeth started chattering.

"Making things. I sewed by hand an elaborate wardrobe for a red-haired doll I had. There was a Singer store in our neighborhood, and my thrill was to buy clothes patches they sold to quilt makers, ten cents each square, all kinds of patterns and colors. What was left over from the red-haired doll's wardrobe I'd use for collages, just elaborate designs of snips of fabric pasted onto shirt cardboard. I also used to make little tableaux out of pipe cleaners, cloth, crepe paper, and I'd give these to my grandfather. One was Jack and Jill next to a well, Jack on the ground with his broken crown — a big red gash across his head — Jill holding the pail, looking horrified.

"Baking fascinated me for a long time. I used to make cakes and cookies, and deliver these little packages to neighbors."

MAX, 58
vice president with a food company

"As I said, I was the little comedian. When I started seriously wondering if I could write for some of the comedy shows on TV, I actually began a joke book and laboriously typed out my gags, thinking I could send them some-where. Sid Caesar was going to buy this stuff!

"It was always show biz. I could have fit into one of those forties musicals where everybody runs around say-ing, 'Let's put on a play!' I'd get my brothers doing Marx Brothers routines, me of course as Groucho."

SHEILA, 55
senior partner in a law firm

"I loved to read and write. As soon as I could read, I always had a book under way, mostly fiction, detective stories, and later poetry and short stories. Then I started writing plays the summer I first went to sleepaway camp. The camp director would let me put them on.

"One play was about a prince who drowned in a tidal wave. Another was something about a turtle and a pig. I kept on writing these little plays and then short stories all through elementary school and high school. College, too. I have a theory that law school takes the creativity out of people — I know in my case I stopped writing creatively at that point, with the need to focus so exclusively on ra-tional and analytical thinking.

"I think I still have several scrapbooks with all those plays I wrote.

"Also, as a kid I was extremely religious. I had a great belief in God, in spirituality. I went to religious camps and after-school studies, and loved it."

BARRY, 66
investor, consultant, arts critic, retired manufacturer

"I was addicted to my radio programs. This was my routine — every night at seven I'd get a glass of milk and a
box of Mr. Salty pretzel sticks, sit right in front of my
radio, and listen to my shows. Jack Armstrong, the Green
Hornet, the Lone Ranger, one after the other. When they
were finished, I'd go to bed. Did this for years.

"My other addictions. I had a Sunday morning ritual.
I'd take subway fare and a little money for food, leave
about nine-thirty, get on the subway, and explore every
mile of the New York City transit system. Every stop from
the Bronx to Queens, standing in the front car and looking
out the window. To her credit, as impossible as she was, my
mother used to let me go everywhere.

"Then, baseball. When I was about twelve, I became a
rabid Brooklyn Dodgers fan. I'd go to the games by myself, get there early, and when they opened the gates, run
like hell to get in the first row in the bleachers.

"I had a coin collection. It still pains me to think that
I sold that in college for one-fiftieth of what it was probably worth, to get some cash for that semester."

THERESA, 58
retired management supervisor in an oil company

"I really had no hobbies or special interests. To tell you the
truth, I don't think I had time for them. I was like all good
little Italian girls, looking after the house.

"For a while I liked to paint pictures. My mother

frowned on this kind of thing, however. She told me I had 'creative corners,' which was not good, because 'that's where the devil hides.' Sometimes I wonder if she ruined me for life!"

DAVE, 64
retired talent agent

"I would say I had serial hobbies. Something that caught my eye for a while. I wasn't any good with my hands or playing sports, so that was a drawback. As a very young kid, I used to tear out maps from *National Geographic,* tape them to my walls, and just indulge in these escape daydreams. I'd stare at the maps and imagine myself anywhere else except where I was.

"But the main thing always was anything to do with the theater, acting, especially motion pictures. I'd go whenever I could. This was another form of escape, I believe, putting myself somewhere else, or into another persona."

MAY, 84
psychologist in private practice

"I loved playing house, collecting dolls. I was an ordinary little girl. Later on, I did become seriously interested in photography."

◆ ◆ ◆

While you were still a young child dreaming your fantasies and pursuing your passions, most other life choices probably were seldom yours to make. Your primary goals and life patterns were largely externally set by parents and the other adults in your life: now you will start school (they let it be known), these are the grades we expect you to earn, here are the family obligations you must meet. But also conveyed, in all likelihood, were more subliminal messages concerning the value and meaning of work, for example, and the relative importance of private interests and pleasures.

Think about the messages promoted in your childhood home. If you have brothers or sisters, take a sibling reading; talk to them about memorable moments and messages from that time, and get their shadings on your joint kid life. Consider, especially, questions having to do with work:

- In your family, was the prevailing impression that work was a drudgery to be endured, or a worthy effort to be relished?
- Was one job as good as any other, as long as it provided steady work and a steady income?
- From the adults in your life, did you receive specific advice, or vague impressions about all this?

Leo M., head of his own small accounting firm, remembered his father drilling into him one thought: "He'd say, 'Leo, I don't care what you do in life, but whatever it is, work for yourself! Don't work for anybody else! That's the way to misery!' He was so heated on this score, I'm sure, because he had had his own company in the garment business that he lost in the Depression, and then he had to work for his brother's company, which drove him crazy. My mother was a lovely woman but not very bright or very independent, and this matter of my father's being employed by my uncle caused her a lot of grief because it clearly caused my father a lot of grief. He worked hard but unhappily. So we lived within an aura of his dissatisfaction and grief." Leo thinks osmosing the work-for-yourself lesson from an early age had a lot to do with his own career decisions.

Read what our eight friends had to say about their own family gestalts, as you go back to your spiral notebook and start a new page:

LESSONS ON THE HOME FRONT

JACK, 58
school guidance counselor

"Work was of the essence. My father ran a small women's clothing shop, and I used to help out there during summers and school breaks. I watched him pull out twenty dresses or blouses to try to make one sale, and then lots of times the customer left without buying anything. He opened early in the morning, six days a week, and closed at eight or nine at night. He was always beat."

Jack's mother didn't hold a job outside the home, but "the housework seemed endless, and she was always going at it in a grim sort of way. Twice a year we kids had to help her take up the carpets and beat them on a line outside. Then all the furniture had to go back exactly where it had been. She was always cooking, baking, doing laundry, going to my grandparents' place and helping them out. Once, maybe twice a year we'd all get in the car and drive to a picnic ground at the public park. That would be our fun.

"All us kids had to start working, for money, at very young ages. When I consider my siblings today, I know that we all shared the same perception. They both work all the time, just like me. And I'm not sure they like what they're doing. But liking it wasn't ever the point."

ISABELLA, 45
*communications director for a medical
equipment manufacturer*

A self-described "precocious little brain," Isabella entered college at age sixteen. Her adored late father ran a prosperous printing company while thinking he probably could have been a professor of English literature.

"Reading endlessly, then discussing and debating the merits of various writers, that's what he loved," she said. "Education was the highest value. I think my overachieving passage through school had a lot to do with wanting him to beam at his wonderful daughter." Her three sisters — each married, each now the mother of three children — and her brother all were equally bright students.

"Dad was intellectual. Mom was sensuous," said Isabella. "She was a great cook, fantastic gardener, did a lot of charity work. She was also a serious craftsperson and made lots of weavings and really beautiful, small decorative things for the house."

They were enormously hardworking, "but both of them were kind of unhelpful, in a way. We kids knew we *had* to do well in school, because poor grades meant that you just weren't working enough. So we had very strong messages about the importance of education, and yet my sisters and I weren't especially encouraged to think in terms of careers. My mother thought teaching was a 'nice' profession, which meant you could probably always get a job. Also, that you could go into it and then leave it at any time, when you started a family.

"The message was conveyed in many small ways, that for us girls work was sort of temporary and that it was a mistake to overeducate yourself, because you'd scare off the guys. So it was a somewhat schizophrenic message."

MAX, 58
vice president with a food company

His father, said Max, prided himself on being "a father of sons, four boys. Boys were good. Girls were cute and fun, but not much good. Boys were good because they went out and worked and took care of the family, which was my father's role in life.

"He had probably about twenty jobs over his lifetime, sometimes three or four at once, maybe not all of them strictly kosher. He was a hustling, laboring, hardworking guy. He worked on the docks, in the meat district, as a track inspector for the railroad, construction work, opened restaurants later on. He expected his sons to go that route, and my brothers basically did. I was pretty much the odd-ball in that crowd, because I liked school, for one thing."

SHEILA, 55
senior partner in a law firm

Both her parents, Sheila says, were fierce liberals — "radicalized Democrats, committed to the need for social change."

Both parents, too, were discontented with their own professional choices, or lack thereof: "My mother never finished college, held a series of jobs but wasn't really trained for anything, and desperately wanted to be a creative writer. She took lots of classes, did lots of writing, but never had anything published. My father was a podiatrist, hated it, and was always looking around to see if there was something else he could do. And he was stymied — he got to that point where he was making too much money to switch, and he didn't know what to switch to anyway."

Their own example, "both of them caring passionately about politics in the global sense, and both of them unhappy with their own work," conveyed a powerful message, Sheila said: "First, make the world a better place and second, find something to do that you really love, because otherwise you'll be bored and frustrated and miserable. But it was never pressure toward a particular area of work. The question was what I would do with my life."

BARRY, 66
investor, consultant, arts critic, retired manufacturer

"My mother and I were on our own, and she was often sick. My father was gone before I was a year old, and I never met him. I knew we were poor. We were on welfare some of the time; I knew that, too.

"I was always working. The year I was twelve, I ran a glazier's shop for the whole summer. Took the calls for two glaziers, took care of scheduling appointments, learned how to cut glass in the back. I didn't know twelve-year-olds don't know that stuff.

"From age ten, I delivered groceries at night for four or five dollars. The year I was thirteen, I worked seventy hours a week in a candy store. The owner, who had a fabulous deal in me, used to begrudge me a free milk shake in the afternoon. So, I always worked, but I don't remember any messages on the home front about it all."

THERESA, 58
retired management supervisor in an oil company

To say that work was important in her household, Theresa said, "would be an understatement. My father died when we kids were still pretty young. Our mother always had jobs. When I wasn't in school or doing schoolwork, as I said, I was supposed to take care of the house, start the dinner.

"Five years after I started my job, I got a little award for never being out once in that time, and I remember my mother was so proud of that. That was it, even when I was back in school. If I said, 'Ma, I don't feel very well today, can't I stay home?' she'd say, 'You're fine, go to school.' Never be absent, always show up on time, do what they tell you to do."

DAVE, 64
retired talent agent

"The lessons were crystal clear: 'We must work. We must work all the time. We must look over our shoulders because people are going to try to cut us out. The world is a hostile and dangerous place, and we must watch our moves every step of the way. Someone is going to take something away from you, or get the better of you, or exploit you. People are lined up behind you, ready to go for what you want.'

"That came from my father, that was his take on his own life. And from both my parents I got the impression that I'd never have any real money, because I was too much of a daydreamer."

Work was never meant to be something one enjoyed, Dave said: "The idea was, find something that you're good enough at so that you can earn a living and keep the wolf from the door. This notion that you should find what you loved to do was nonexistent. I never heard anybody say, 'Be what you want to be.'"

MAY, 84
psychologist in private practice

"Messages on the home front . . . there were a lot. My mother was a workaholic. She came here from Austria with her parents and six siblings when she was in her mid-teens, the oldest child, and then her mother died about a year later. I always felt she never really got over that, all the responsibility that landed on her.

"She ran my father's business, always at her desk, adding up figures. A serious, serious woman, not much of a sense of humor, no good at sports or card games or just relaxing. Her one indulgence was that she adored opera, especially Wagner, and she had a little group of two or three friends who loved that music, too. I called them the Wagner Hens. They'd get together and play the recordings through and then start them over again. The rest of the time she just worked.

"On the other hand, maybe not surprisingly, she didn't wish for me to follow in her footsteps at all. She didn't want me to have a career, or even go to college. She wanted me to, you know, be a nice girl, find a nice man. Sit back and sigh and play the piano."

◆ ◆ ◆

Continue to recollect what captured your attention and colored your life during Act One. Write down the names of individuals who made a powerful impression on you, whom you admired or saw fit to emulate. That may have been a parent or other close relative. Said James F., a stock trader: "My father was not a particularly emotional person, not real good with his kids. I don't know that he ever told me he loved me. But he was such a neat individual. Not very tall, but he just had a remarkable aura of success and confidence surrounding him. You could have a chat with him, and whatever you were talking about, you could go to the bank on what he told you. I always tried to model that aura of confidence and reliability."

Perhaps it was a schoolteacher, priest, or sports figure

who struck you as out of the ordinary, someone to look up to, learn from, or like. Consider:

- Were your heroes noteworthy for their warmth, humor, and generosity?
- For their looks and style?
- For a quality of bravery and derring-do?
- Were they outstanding competitors, or contributors to a particular field or activity you thought was worthwhile?
- Did you spend time with them, or admire from a distance?

Try to come up with three or four of your own most memorable people and describe what made them remarkable to your young self on the next page in your notebook:

MY HEROES, MY FAVORITE OR MOST UNFORGETTABLE PEOPLE

JACK, 58
school guidance counselor

"There was Mantle, of course. That man could swing a bat! And he was awesome in the outfield. I wanted to be him.

"My uncle Ed would definitely be one of my unforgettable people. He had been in the navy for years, and then after that he worked in some international kind of business. He'd visit us a couple of times a year and tell great stories about traveling around the world. Once when he was staying with us, we all took a bus trip to the shore for a day, and after swimming in the ocean, Uncle Ed said he wouldn't take a shower because he enjoyed the feeling left by the salt water on his skin. In the navy, apparently, they used to bathe in seawater. I remember thinking that was so exciting. Uncle Ed would take the time to look at my stamps, and he'd tell me stories about these different countries. He seemed so worldly!

"Mr. Cole, my high school English teacher. He was so great with us kids. Everyone loved him. And he found literature so interesting, he even made us enjoy it. I think I went into teaching because of him."

ISABELLA, 45
communications director for a medical equipment manufacturer

"My older brother was my hero because he was so solid, focused, always seemed to know what he wanted out of life and where he was going. And he was really a brilliant student, which I think has a lot to do with why my sisters and I worked at being academic bright lights. I tried to be like my brother.

"Nancy Drew, if you can have a fictional hero. Oh, the longing to have Nancy's life!"

MAX, 58
vice president with a food company

"My heroes were the funny men I admired from the distance. Sid Caesar, Mel Brooks, Jackie Gleason. Even Gary Moore.

"But my truly most unforgettable people were all the old characters in my huge family, my grandparents, great uncles and aunts, their assorted cronies in the neighborhood. *Characters* is the word for them! They were uneducated people, manual jobs. And they were just vivid, bold in every way — they radiated energy. Outsize personalities.

"They didn't get mad, they got furious! Raging! They didn't get sad, they got miserable, they cried big tears, they hung on to each other's necks. At family parties and neighborhood things, everybody sang, everybody danced. And they all had amazing, hard stories to tell. I was fascinated by them.

"I felt more like ten generations away from these people, not two, my activities, my emotions were just so different. Not necessarily better."

SHEILA, 55
senior partner in a law firm

"As a very young kid, nobody much was a hero, except my parents and especially my mother. She was a feminist before the word existed. She certainly believed women were equal or superior to men. I admired her tremendously. My mother made me think that I was somebody special, with special talents, but all the while she never pushed me in any one direction. I think now that was pretty remarkable of her. That's where my drive came from, in some way.

"Later, Eleanor Roosevelt. A couple of my professors. Adlai Stevenson, because he was so brilliant. JFK, a hero of mine in law school. I think my heroes were all men and women who were great liberals and either achieved great social goals or at least talked a good game."

BARRY, 66
investor, consultant, arts critic, retired manufacturer

"My earliest heroes were the guys I heard on the radio —
Jack Armstrong, the Lone Ranger, the Green Hornet.
They were all he-men and they all did powerful things.
They'd get tortured by the Nazis or whatever, and they
handled it. They were larger than life.

"Later, my heroes became real people. The hero of heroes for me was Jackie Robinson. He wasn't the best
player, never a Ted Williams. But he was so aggressive, always looking for that little competitive edge. Twice I saw
him steal. And there is no play in baseball more exciting
or more difficult than stealing. I watched him faking his
way back to the base to slow the pitcher down, a big,
bulky guy, bowlegged as hell, and he looked funny running. And yet, better runners couldn't steal bases as fast.
My thinking now is, he played the game the way I'd like
to play the game."

THERESA, 58
retired management supervisor in an oil company

"Joe DiMaggio, I think first because he was Italian. But
then I realized he was a great ballplayer, and I loved baseball.

"My older sister — she died a few years ago, in her forties — was a hero to me. She was my crutch, very bright,
very accomplished. I tried to be like her, but I never
thought I measured up."

DAVE, 64
retired talent agent

"Cary Grant. Gary Cooper. I can't remember trying to be *like* anybody, or thinking that I'd grow up to be that kind of person."

MAY, 84
psychologist in private practice

"My childhood heroes all had to do with my mother's passion for music, especially German opera. She started taking me to the opera at an early age, and I adored some of the singers — Rosa Ponselle, for one. And then my aunt, my mother's older sister, married a Viennese guy whose brother was a concert violinist. And *he* married a young singer who became a great Wagnerian soprano at the Met. So these slightly removed aunts and uncles of mine made up a very glamorous, delightful, romantic group of people, all very exciting to me as a young girl.

"None of them, however, had any impact on my plans for the future."

◆　◆　◆

The beginning of the end of Act One in your life story coincides with the conclusion of your formal education. For all the people interviewed here, the end of schooling (usually college or graduate school, law school, or medical school) marked the great divide from child (teenager, youth, student) to what the world deemed an adult — and that is one you, too, probably remember most vividly.

Before the great divide, you were, to one extent or another, cared for and dictated to by others; after, you were suddenly your own man or woman in significant ways — expected to get your own job, find your own place to live, secure your own health insurance, and so on. Reflect back now to that point at which you were teetering on the line between before and after, the several years during which you pursued and completed your education and anticipated your work life to come.

As you remember the beginning of college, it's probably clear that suddenly, then, you were living life on a larger stage; suddenly, for the first time, much of it was tossed right in your lap. Decisions and choices had to be made, and you had something to do with making them.

Cast your thoughts back to your realistic ("I've got to pick a major") stage.

Focus on the decisions and choices, and how they seem to you now:

- Did you pick the college you would attend, go where your best friend was going, or accede to your parents' or some other adult's wishes?
- If you roomed in a dormitory, was all that togetherness with people your own age enjoyable, or not especially to your liking?
- Did you study what you loved, or what you thought would prepare you for a good job, or were the two the same?

The wildly successful "Far Side" cartoonist Gary Larson planned to major in biology but switched to what he thought was a more useful degree in communications, a decision he called years later "one of the most idiotic things I ever did." Entomology, he said, "is my fantasy, the road not taken."[10]

Then think about the moment you stepped over the divide, at graduation or the completion of professional studies, a passage that may have contained the seeds of a number of possibilities, the first real forks in the road.

♦ If you were to return to that time and start again, would you elect to try another fork in the road?

Sarah S., a social worker, found herself thinking of that time as a significant turning point. She had graduated from college in 1960, the year the Peace Corps was created; one of her close friends joined and, as it happened, was photographed along with others in that premier group for *Life* magazine. Sarah was startled by the intensity of her memory of that image: "I can still see the picture of my friend in *Life,* sitting at a desk filling out forms. I thought it was brave and amazing for her to do that. I was envious."

Impulsively, she herself applied for a two-year teaching position in South America, a notion she let her parents talk her out of. "I haven't thought about that in years," Sarah said, "but I remember being so excited and then so let down, by myself. I should have taken that teaching job."

♦ And when college was over, did you feel ready for Act Two of your life?

Stan L., a lawyer with a state department of justice, remembered his four years of college as a passage from "absolute certainty to a large question mark. I grew up assuming I'd go into my father's insurance business in our town. So I went to the university as a business major, started to get a broader vision of the world and life, realized that no way could I go back home. I remember very distinctly completing my undergraduate years thinking, number one, insurance is out, and number two, I feel as though I don't know anything. I can't be of any value to anybody. So I need more education. And number three, All right, what do I do?"

Start a new page in your notebook, with the heading:

COLLEGE DAYS: THE PLUSES AND THE MINUSES

JACK, 58
school guidance counselor

"I went to a nearby college and commuted from home. My parents didn't go to college and didn't have much to offer on the subject. I don't remember talking to anyone at school about various possibilities. Money was the main factor in my choice. I guess it was essentially a nonchoice.

"I picked my major, I think, because of Mr. Cole, that teacher everybody liked. I had no idea what I wanted to be — baseball player being out of the question by then! I wasn't the greatest student, and the ed courses didn't seem too difficult.

"If I had another shot at it, I think I'd major in something about international issues, world geography, economics maybe. Something more expansive and less sheltered than teaching."

ISABELLA, 45
*communications director for a medical
equipment manufacturer*

"I applied to just one college, very academically elite, because my brother and older sister went there. I knew I'd get in, and it was the only place I wanted to go. Very overly confident, I was. I did get in, I did exceptionally well, and my courses were all over the map — calculus, Spanish, French, art history, a preponderance of literature classes, which meant I ended up with an English major. Which I had no plan to do anything with after I graduated."

MAX, 58
vice president with a food company

"I was the first one in my family to go to college, a free city school. But going to college was in no way encouraged or even admired. My father was that macho guy with his sons, if you were a *real* man, you were out of your parents' house and on the street hustling when you hit, like, age fifteen, which is what he did. So there was no big 'my son, the college student' kind of pride at home. He made it clear that he thought so much education was a waste of good time, even though the man wasn't paying for any of it.

"College took me down a peg. There were a lot of really smart kids there. Poor but studious and superbright. Kids who you knew were going to do things in life. So that wasn't so comfortable for me. Plus I never really liked any of the teachers much — a supercilious bunch. I actually hand it to myself that I stuck it out, because there were a lot of reasons for me to chuck it.

"I was your run-of-the-mill English major. In retrospect, psychology would have been a better choice. Actually, when I think about it now, maybe my father had the right idea. Forget all this education. Lots of the great comedians and comic writers just went straight for that when they were still basically kids."

SHEILA, 55
senior partner in a law firm

"For me, the last two years of high school far surpassed anything that came after. I would say that was the point in life when I absolutely loved who I was. I was cute, popular, had loads of friends, boyfriends. I was a great student; all the teachers adored me. I was involved in all the activities. At graduation I got the award for the most successful senior in the class. I thought, 'Oh boy, I'm hot! I'm really going far!' And I was still in my I'm-going-to-change-the-world phase.

"Then came college. I had no particular place in mind, which seems odd to me now. My parents, sophisticated as they were, were not really into where you should go, the 'best' schools and so on. I had no clue what I wanted to study, although I knew my mother would have loved me to become a writer. So I went to a college near home, and it was extremely boring because it was like a continuation of high school classes. Then I found out sort of accidentally that anybody who did well on the LSAT test could get accepted into law school after three years in college. Law school was the same price, and I thought it might be more fun — something different, lots of guys, few women. So I went for it.

"Then I got excited again. This was the time of the women's movement, civil rights, antiwar, and I became very caught up in all those trends. Also, I had two wonderful professors — one who was involved in attempting to establish international police forces and new mechanisms for world order, another who was passionate about civil rights and liberties litigation. So I thought, Yeah, this is for me, very socially conscious kind of law.

"Would I do it again? Probably not. The best part of law for me, as it turned out, was being in law school, with the emotions running high."

BARRY, 66
investor, consultant, arts critic, retired manufacturer

"Two big events in high school got me started. First, I found music. In front of my little radio, twirling the dial, I discovered some jazz and blues programs, and I became an avid listener, during my homework, after homework, in between the Lone Ranger and the others. You listen to something a few times, and you hear a little more each time. In my last year I worked as the music-effects man at a local station — they did radio dramas, and I'd find the music that fit the mood and the transitions. I can't play anything myself, but I started loving anything to do with music, performance.

"Second, the guidance counselor in high school said, 'What are your plans for college?' I said, 'I'm on welfare, I'm not going to college, I need to learn a skill and go to work.' But he urged me to try a bunch of things. They didn't have any electronics courses or lab, which was my dream, but I tried chemistry and became fascinated with it. I had three years of it.

"Started at City for one semester, then I went to the counselor and argued that I shouldn't have to take the required humanities courses, said I wanted to be a biochemist, and look at what I did in chemistry in high school. So they changed the rules for me, and I could stay on. In the second two years, I did a music minor. Got an honorable mention in a National Science Foundation grant, which got me a year's free tuition at graduate school. I did the whole college and grad school thing on my own.

"I wouldn't change any of it."

THERESA, 58
retired management supervisor in an oil company

"I had started working at the company as a typist when I was in high school, during summers and school breaks, and kept on there when I started college. I went to a local college, with a major in elementary education. I had to pay for this myself, so I started working full-time in the office and doing a lot of night classes. I had a three point eight average after the first year, but I was exhausted keeping everything going, so I quit college after a year and never went back."

DAVE, 64
retired talent agent

"Where I went to college had nothing to do with who I was or what I needed, although I did have a strong sense of what would be best for me. I wanted to go to a small place. In fact, I did a fair amount of checking around and I fell in love with several small schools, like four hundred guys in a place up on a hill. I knew in my heart some school like that was right, where I thought I'd be recognized and get some personal attention.

"My parents were very precise about their expectations — it would be Harvard, Yale, or Princeton. 'You should know that,' they said, 'there's no surprise. Any parent who has a child who could go to Harvard would of course insist that child go to Harvard,' and so on and so on. I was allowed to apply only to those three schools, all of which I got into. And I went to Princeton, which was absolutely the wrong place for me. But the choice was made by my parents, because of their notion of what constituted a successful son.

"I chose my major, which was drama. This was violently opposed by my parents, and I had to fight for it like a warrior. Drama was my only salvation, the chance to escape what I found to be a terribly competitive, unfriendly environment. Still, it was essentially a miserable four years."

MAY, 84
psychologist in private practice

"I lived at home and commuted. This was the only way I could possibly manage college, not so much because of the money but because my mother didn't like the whole idea of college in the first place. So this was a compromise.

"But that was just the beginning for me. I got my B.A. at age twenty-one and my Ph.D. at age fifty-one. So my official education went on for a very long time!"

◆ ◆ ◆

Coming up next, the real world — job decisions, living decisions, job changes, living changes, and all the other aspects of full-fledged adulthood. Before opening that chapter of your autobiography, take some time to ponder the journey you have sketched out, from wanting to be an astronaut to having to pick a major.

Although, especially toward the end, you had work to do and grades to achieve, it was a stretch when you had few limitations on your prospects and few responsibilities to others, a stretch of relative freedom that may not be duplicated again until your after-the-job days. How you felt about freedom, unlimited prospects, and the lack of obligations back then may be a clue to how you'll feel about them in the future. And we're hunting for clues.

CHAPTER 5

FROM GETTING A JOB
TO HAVING ARRIVED:
The World of Work

e look now at the central core of your life that started once your formal education ended. For most individuals, that was the busiest of all busy times, years that probably assembled around three broad chunks and associated developmental tasks.

The world of work began with your first job, right out of high school or college, or after medical school, law school, or other advanced studies — a job you had prepared for with enthusiasm, one you fell into by accident, or one you thought sounded at least somewhat up your alley. It intensified during the career-oriented and family-building middle years, when you got down to your appointed business, whatever that was. And it came to rest with a midlife sense of being to some degree or other, "established," of having reached the point beyond which no further major moves seemed likely — the point you may be at right now.

So we'll record in your notebook a summary of that broad swath in your autobiography so far, zeroing in on significant steps through the world of work and how you took them, on what went according to plan or came about without much plan at all, on what you liked or disliked or did well or not so well. From those highlights and impressions we will gather more clues that will be useful as you design what comes next.

◆ ◆ ◆

Remembering back to his first after-school days, Joe R., a teacher of the deaf, described "the years from age twenty-two to twenty-eight as perpetual Sturm und Drang. I skipped through four jobs, each completely different. First, I helped run a program for disabled kids, because I wanted to do something worthwhile and I thought I'd be good working with children, but I made peanuts and couldn't support myself. I took a spot with an ad agency and made decent money, but I couldn't stand myself doing that work. Then I went into business with my uncle and cousin who ran a supply company in the medical field, because I knew it would make the family happy. It didn't make me happy."

During that time, Joe felt "like a loser, a guy who was never going to grow up. I envied my brother Mac, because he knew from day one he was going to be a doctor. He was good in sciences, our father is a doctor, and it was always pretty much assumed Mac would go that route." Today, years after those decisions were made, said Joe, "I love what I do. I'm not so sure Mac loves what he does. He gets a lot of pumping up ego-wise, but he's always talking about when he can quit practicing medicine, which strikes me as kind of odd for a doctor."

In relating those earliest experiences, Joe in essence described common routes into the world of work, involving issues of crisis and commitment. During the five or six years he worried that he was "never going to grow up" and wrestled with possibilities — searching for the right mix among personal values, family wishes, money needs; coming up with some answers but no clear vision — Joe was in what some psychologists call a state of moratorium, going through crisis but having no sense yet of commitment to one particular area.

All the wrestling, including trying several roles on for size, led in time to "identity achievement" for Joe, a satisfactory answer about what kind of work he really wanted. After a time of crisis came commitment.

Brother Mac, it would seem, settled early on into a state of "foreclosure." Mac "always knew" where he was going, but although that decision apparently meshed well with his scientific smarts, he may not have given much consideration to whether he was headed into a career that suited the whole man. While Mac was relieved of the turbulence and discomfort of crisis, he accepted a commitment that was perhaps largely imposed from without.

Identity achievement — the successful accomplishment of Erikson's most critical task for the young adult — doesn't come easily or quickly. According to some statistics, only about half of people in their early postcollege years are satisfied they've pulled together all the disparate pieces into a satisfying plan. (And even by their mid-thirties, almost one in three men — and a somewhat lower percentage of women — are still testing the waters, trying to decide exactly what they want to do; about the same number actually change not just jobs but career fields between the ages of twenty-five and thirty-six.)

For many of us, moratorium was the defining state of our out-of-the-nest-but-not-yet-flying youth — which, in retrospect, we might realize was not so bad. Commitment, settling on a chosen path, without a healthy dose of exploratory crisis doesn't necessarily bode well, and young people who float a number of trial balloons are the ones most likely to come up finally with sound, suitable, happy choices. Moratorium also need not necessarily have been full of Sturm und Drang. For some, feeling puzzled on the road to identity prompted bold experimentation, creativity, even playfulness, before getting down to the serious stuff of adulthood.

Roger B., a lawyer turned businessman, remembered his own early career days as a wide-open expanse full of possibilities: "I was pretty good at a lot of things, starting back in high school, none of them especially connected. At my Jesuit school, if you didn't want to take a third year of Greek, you could take chemistry, so I got chemistry only because I didn't want more Greek. Then I skipped senior year and went straight into a Jesuit college, on a full chemistry scholarship. This was when kids who maybe were going for science careers got a lot of financial support.

There I started to do some writing, and I found that I liked it and I was good at it. I also hung out with the theater group, painting sets and so on. Out of college, I packed up my beakers, with no idea what I wanted to do."

So, working all the while as a bench chemist to support himself, Roger "took two years off to dabble. I took an English course and studio painting classes. I applied for a chemistry graduate program and decided against that at the last minute. I talked to some of my old professors about going for a master's in writing and got as far as filling out the applications. At the same time I took the law boards, did fine, and decided to go back to school that way, largely because of thoughts of financial security. So my first job was always very consciously about paying the rent until I figured things out."

Think about your own first forays into the work world, and how — or if — you struggled with issues of crisis and commitment and answers to "who am I and what do I want out of life?" Some questions you might consider:

- Did you choose your first job intentionally, or take what was available?
- Did you give yourself freedom to experiment?
- Did you go for the safe and sure, or the brash and brave?
- Did you follow a path dictated by family expectations? Or one in revengeful rejection of those expectations?
- Were your earliest job experiences exciting and exhilarating, or disappointing and discouraging?

Jot down your thoughts on a new page in your notebook:

My First Job — What and Why

JACK, 58
school guidance counselor

"When I got out of college, there were a lot of teaching jobs available. I applied in towns close to home, and took a job actually in the town I grew up in.

"It felt comfortable — this was the school system I went to, so I sort of knew my way around in some ways."

ISABELLA, 45
communications director for a medical
equipment manufacturer

"I got out of college with my English-major liberal-arts degree, without a clue of what comes next. You're barreling along through all those years of school, and then suddenly it all stops cold.

"From my parents, I was always absorbing those vague notions that I should be a teacher, so I thought of myself as possibly teaching language in a high school, because I was good in languages. I even applied for a master of arts in teaching program my senior year in college. Then it suddenly dawned on me that this would be a very dull job, that teaching language is just drill, and the best way to learn a language is probably to go to the country and start speaking it. Also, all my favorite French and Spanish teachers were what we used to call spinsters, and they were all, I thought, doing pretty thankless work.

"So, after college I decided to have a little adventure,

and I went to Paris and got a job as a secretary at a film company. Stayed there for two great years, and I developed this notion of being secretary to a United States senator maybe, or some other very important person. I didn't think of myself as really doing my own thing as much as being support staff to some great person. Then that didn't sound terribly exciting, either.

"I came home and then I got really nervous. I went to an employment agency for 'college grads,' which had two jobs available that day. One was working for a company that manufactured corn products, which seemed less than thrilling. The other was an entry-level training position at a publishing house — we were called 'floaters'— and I took it.

"Why? Panic — I had to get something. No better idea. My father, I knew, would be tickled that his little girl was working in what he considered a prestigious business. Plus, a vague notion of living a glamorous life."

MAX, 58
vice president with a food company

"Straight out of college I headed to the big TV networks, filled out their job-application forms, and basically said I'd take anything they had. I thought being a page would be pretty fantastic, but I would have been happy to sweep floors. I was going to get my foot in that door.

"Nothing happened for about eight or nine months. I did bartending, dog walking, borrowed a friend's van and hauled furniture around for people, just to make some bucks. Meanwhile, I was calling the studios once a week, making a pest of myself. Finally, I was offered a job in the mailroom at one of the networks, sorting and delivering, forty dollars a week. I was ecstatic!

"It was just what I wanted, my entrée to show business. I had no doubt I was on my way."

SHEILA, 55
senior partner in a law firm

"My first job out of law school was as a public defender. Not exactly what I had in mind, but it was making the world a more just place in some small way, it seemed to me.

"Mainly, though, it was all I could get. At the end of law school, I went around for interviews, several in Washington — with the Agency for International Development and some others. I was thinking also of the Justice Department, maybe the State Department, maybe something at the United Nations. And wherever I went, it was pretty much the same — they were all hiring from the Ivy League, which I wasn't. So my dream of doing something in international law kind of blew away.

"Why that public defender job? It was reality time, work or no work."

BARRY, 66
investor, consultant, arts critic, retired manufacturer

"With my M.S. in chemistry, I took the first job that came up, as a research chemist in a new installation in Pennsylvania. They had hired about two thousand engineers and technicians to create this monstrous facility, everything from atomic power to jet engine development. Shortly after I got there, management changed, there was nothing for us to do, and I wound up sitting in a bull pen with a bunch of very bright Ph.D.'s.

"It sounded just right for me, research in chemistry. But they pulled the plug on me. That started me down some different roads."

THERESA, 58
retired management supervisor in an oil company

"I started out as a clerk, and really I felt right at home from the start. It was a very tightly run, disciplined place. Plus they went according to a real apprenticeship system, so I figured I could learn a lot from my supervisor and eventually work up to that level.

"I never looked around for another job, because I'd been at this company during my high school summers, and I knew it."

DAVE, 64
retired talent agent

"At the time I got out of my one year of grad school and started thinking career, I was not psychologically strong enough to follow my dream about theater and to resist the enormous pressures that came from the voices of my parents, the way they raised me, the whole push for a salary and a white picket fence. So basically, I moved a hundred and eighty degrees away from theater and all the people involved with that, and took on an essentially mechanical job, editing a trade magazine for the commercial lighting business.

"Why? I could make a living. And it wasn't all bad, because I acquired some good skills, a good command of the language. When I made my big, striking-out-from-home stab at life, moving to California a couple of years later, I ended up there in a think tank, writing and editing manuals. I had the organizational and expressive skills required. It was okay but never what I was after."

MAY, 84
psychologist in private practice

"Out of college I got a job at a county psychiatric institute, helping a psychiatrist write up his research. He turned out to be a horrible creature, actually, who fudged his stuff. At the same time, I was dealing with my mother's anxiety about my working in this place. I always had a really hard time with my mother concerning my interests. So I quit that after three months, no regrets.

"Then I took a teaching assistant spot at a women's college in the Northeast, hated every minute of it. They told me to get a room in the graduate students' dorm, and I went there and found there was no one I would want to say hello to. These were blue stockings of the dull variety. So I rented a room in town, which was better, and started doing some testing work also with the local school districts.

"It was all of a piece. I always knew I was going to be a practicing therapist. And I knew these jobs were on the road to that, although they were not too pleasurable."

❖ ❖ ❖

Take a giant leap forward now from those first forays, tentative or secure, across the rest of your working life. Perhaps, as was the case with many of the individuals who described their job paths to me, your career followed a traditional linear pattern, working for one employer and moving if not always upward at least onward within a single corporate structure. "I grew up in that old style, cradle-to-grave work environment," said one such individual, a plant supervisor. "You come in, put your nose to the grindstone, do a good job, and you'll prove yourself worthy of promotional consideration. Management decides when it's time for you to move on."

Or you worked for three or four companies within the same field, jumping up a notch each time in title and responsibility.

Or perhaps you skipped here and there, and experienced several twists and turns.

In all likelihood, the drives, efforts, and expectations that defined the early rungs on your particular ladder evolved into something very different by the end. In their study "Work, Careers and Aging," psychologists David Karp and William Yoels describe the earliest years as a period of "learning the ropes," figuring out what the job calls for, how the higher-ups judge your performance, where the power lies, and other aspects of being an adult now solidly ensconced in the world of work. At this stage of the game, men and women "sense themselves at the beginning of a journey, the work journey. . . . They are still very much creating themselves, still 'becoming' something.

Theirs is a life trajectory that . . . they view as extending far into the future."

Some years later, by about age forty or forty-five, perhaps you had entered what Karp and Yoels call the "coming to grip" years: "Whatever might have been their private dreams, aspirations, or fantasies, they must now acknowledge the realities of their occupational positions. By mid-life the lawyers who are partners in a small law firm know that they will never sit on the bench as judges; doctors in private practice know that they will not be renowned medical innovators; academics with a few publications know that their names will not be recognized by the great majority of colleagues in their field."[11]

On the other hand, the law firm partner may have gone exactly as far as he had hoped, the doctor never had medical innovator aspirations to begin with, the academic found her talent in teaching rather than publishing, and each enjoyed the gratifying sense of having made the grade.

"Coming to grips" time may be for you outstandingly satisfying years, the time of peak power. Possibly it's a peaceful, stable stretch, when achievement goals once ferociously focused on career building give way in part to maintenance goals or efforts to solidify and retain the status you've already reached.

Somewhere between learning the ropes and coming to grips, you were probably "getting a life" in other ways as well. Perhaps, as is true for many in their mid- or late twenties to mid- or late thirties, you found a love partner, started a family, bought a house. And perhaps, too, whether you are a man or a woman had something to do with the way those years played out for you.

Peter H. was a combined physics and engineering major through college and graduate school. "I did my doctoral work at the University of Illinois, developing models for analysis of temperatures at the earth's core," he said. "I copublished a dozen papers while I was there and had no doubt I'd spend my life in the lab doing pure research, my first love. Right after grad school I took a job at X Company, planned to stay there a couple of years, get some money in the bank and pay off loans, then go back to teaching and research."

He married Annie one year into the job, they had the first of their three children one year after that, the life of a university researcher seemed less tenable, and Peter has been at X Company now for twenty-nine years, most recently as a vice president in the automotive products division. His focus, Peter said, "was ninety-seven percent on the job in the beginning. Now it's down to about seventy-five percent."

The family moved four times, to four different states, as Peter transferred among company divisions on his way up the career ladder. He hasn't had the chance to spend a lot of time with his kids; although he's devoted to them, his fatherly attentions over the years centered on "making sure we lived in a community with a good school district, for one thing, which meant that for one stretch I had a two-hour drive to and from work every day. And making good on the job, so the family would be secure, the kids would have lots of opportunities."

Annie, meanwhile, taught first grade for a couple of years, then stayed home with the children, then bought part ownership of a card and gift shop, helped manage that until they moved and she sold her interest, stayed home again until her third child started kindergarten. Recently, she has reentered the work world as office manager in a private school and is taking courses toward a master's degree in education administration.

Peter and Annie's story is not uncommon. Especially for men and women who began careers thirty or more years ago, gender differences may have strongly influenced how each approached the matter of balancing work and family, and determined where the passion lay. Like many men, Peter settled in his late twenties and early thirties into an intense stage of career consolidation — being "a success" at work was on the front burner and was even the measure by which he deemed himself a good husband and father. According to much research in human development, having a job, performing it successfully, and having that success recognized in economic terms is largely the way men define themselves as masculine and mature.

Which is not to say that men are uninterested in intimacy, and women care little about work identity. From the studies of forty men and their life histories that led to his well-known book *The Seasons of a Man's Life,* the psychologist Daniel Levinson described four primary tasks or activities of what he called the era of early adulthood: finding a dream, a mentor, an occupation, and a love relationship. Several researchers subsequently set out to determine if the same strivings held true for women and concluded that, by and large, they did — with significantly different emphases.

Both men and women have their dreams, search for a suitable occupation, and want to connect with a love partner. But women, they found, have "split dreams," while work is the core aspect for men, with intimacy achievement a kind of add-on: "Men's dreams, which tended to incorporate an image of independent achiever in an occupational role, were fundamentally different from the kind of dream reported by women. Women's dreams contained an image of self-in-adult-world defined in relation to others, such as husbands, children and colleagues." Men formed the "individualistic dream"; women, the "relational dream."[12]

Annie fit that picture — following a more complex, discontinuous path than her husband; accommodating his career goals and changes; dipping in and out of the work world according to the family's priorities; and reaching new career decisions later in life. "I liked having a job outside the house, although we didn't really need my income," Annie said. "But I never felt compelled to 'get ahead' in that way. I'm more ambitious now than I used to be."

Many studies have shown that the push to compete and strive in the workplace, to "get ahead" on a career path, often declines for women during the years they're having and raising the kids — and then may come to the surface again after the family-intense years are past. A few decades ago virtually no woman who was married and a mother also worked at a job without interruption until retirement, not unless she could somehow bend the job to the needs of the family.

A retired physician, now eighty-four, was something of an anomaly for her time. "My father, I think, was unusually enlightened," said Caroline P. "He felt women should get the best possible education, be self-supporting, and he said he'd pay my tuition for whatever I wanted to do, which was to be a doctor, as he was." The first of her four children was born two years after she completed medical school, and Caroline chose her specialty, dermatology, "because it fit in with the children. I could set up a practice at home. It was essentially a little cottage industry." She found the specialty a bit boring: "Acne after acne after acne. But no emergency calls, no night hours. It was good for the family."

The woman without a job or a "cottage industry" who stayed home building the nest and raising the children then often found herself with not much to do when those activities were completed. Annie's mother was such a woman, Annie thought: "Once we kids were gone, her life got very quiet. I think she actually had a pretty ambitious spirit, but no way to use it. She painted the whole house every couple of years. She hand made her own Christmas cards — a very big deal that occupied her for a couple of months out of the year. I don't think she was unhappy, but neither did she seem very satisfied."

Even today, when the majority of women with schoolage children are in the workforce, surveys indicate that their work patterns are different from men's; they take part-time jobs, or drop out for a while, or remove themselves from competitive maneuvers. But later, they see more options than did their mothers — starting a new job, returning to school, running for the Senate.

Reflect back now on your own career path, from the time you were first learning the ropes to the time you came to grips. To paint a picture, invent if you like your version of that old board game Careers — put an X at the lower left hand of a page in your notebook and an X at the upper right hand, and plot out your steps along the way, from where you began to where you had essentially got where you were going. Mark with circles times of transition or change along the way. Give some thought to these turning points and to how they hit you.

Some questions that might be pertinent to your story:

- When did you receive or lose a promotion, turn down a job, get fired?
- Did you at any point take yourself off the job path for a while?
- Did you at any point plunge into the unknown, jump disciplines, leave behind what you knew you did well and try something radically different?
- Was there a point, or more than one, at which you had to adjust to a new boss or owner?
- Was there a point at which you started to think of yourself as part of the old guard, or maybe just old?
- At that point, were you satisfied with the progress you had made?

Your satisfaction or dissatisfaction may have had some connection to a sense of being "on time" — right where you expected to be when you expected to be — or "off time"— not at the level you thought you'd be when big changes could no longer be anticipated.

Maybe you were "ahead of time" — a hot shot who was always on the fast track. For Anthony S., an executive in an ad agency, satisfaction came from measuring himself against coworkers. "I was always looking at how I was doing compared with other people my age," he said. "Was I ahead or behind my class? And having been a kid who skipped a couple of grades in school, I meant to stay ahead.

I liked being out in front, better than the other account managers, moving up faster. And I'm still ahead."

◆ Did you pass the baton to a younger generation? Become a mentor yourself, more advice giver than advice seeker?

Note it all on the next page of your autobiography so far:

MY CAREER-BUILDING YEARS: STEPS, TURNING POINTS, AND TRANSITIONS

JACK, 58
school guidance counselor

"I stayed in the teaching spot for about ten years. I got married, had a couple of kids. I needed more money, so I decided to go for a master's. The university in our city offered two, reading and guidance. I chose guidance and counseling because I didn't want to teach reading to elementary-school kids.

"Once, somewhere in the middle, I left the school and took a job with a corporation in the human resources department, but I got worried about not being able to put in enough time there to qualify for benefits, so I stayed only about a year. Went back to the schools.

"Except for that one detour, my career path is a straight line, but I didn't get as far as I wanted to. I vaguely thought once that I'd be a principal someday. I got the certification, but I never went ahead with it. I never wanted to be in charge. Maybe now that I'm older, I realize that I could have done it."

ISABELLA, 45
communications director for a medical
equipment manufacturer

"I was married at age twenty-four, divorced five years later, and around then I went through a reevaluation process.

"I was still in the book business, working mostly on a paperback line of supplementary reading books for college courses, which I found pretty tedious. A senior editor I really liked had taken an interest in me, we had some lunches together, and she asked me what my plans were, what goals I had. She said, essentially, You're never going to make much money here and there's limited advancement, so you'd better love what you're doing. I realized I didn't love what I was doing very much at all.

"A man I was seeing at that time worked in the communications department of a corporation, and he told me about an opening in publications, doing some speech writing, preparing publicity materials. The money was a whole lot better, so I made the move. That turned out to be a good job for me, because for one thing I got really up to speed on computer skills, designing brochures and so forth. I moved from there to a similar spot in a huge pharmaceuticals company, same work but even better money. I liked those people, especially the scientific people — very smart, dedicated.

"That led to where I am now, in a logical but not especially planned way."

MAX, 58
vice president with a food company

"Show biz, giftwares, Caribbean restaurants, management, that's my checkered path! Crazy!

"I worked like a little beaver in the mailroom, and I got promoted to the cost control department, then got to be a production manager on a drama TV show. I had to hire the makeup and costume people, supervise the props, work out a budget, things like that. I had a single frame credit at the end of the show — 'Production Manager, Max L.' This was fantastic, to be a single guy going to New York parties and having my single frame credit!

"Then for various reasons I started getting the idea that maybe show business wasn't for me. This was a shocker.

"I answered an ad, got what I thought was a temporary job as a giftwares or novelties salesman, ended up selling to shops through four states in the South, then back to the New York district. I tried to get two other jobs in the company, promotion and publicity, but didn't get either, and I was pissed.

"About this time my father and a couple of my brothers were making noises that I should go into the family business, which then was running some restaurants they had down in the islands. And I decided I ought to swallow my pride and get a piece of that business, which was pretty lucrative, so I spent a few years living down there, where on the one hand I learned to relax and on the other hand I started going soft in the head.

"Back to the States. Through the restaurants, I knew some people in the food business who recommended me to the company I'm with now. That was ten years ago. I got staid in my old age. Along the way, I picked up an MBA. Also, I had a couple of marriages in there, which is another story."

SHEILA, 55
senior partner in a law firm

"I was a public defender, a criminal lawyer, a public advocate, a divorce lawyer, a family lawyer, a workers' compensation lawyer. Never left the legal track.

"I don't know if this can be called climbing a career ladder. It was always taking the next thing that seemed available and seemed challenging, so I wouldn't have to stick at something just going through the motions.

"During the time I was occupied with my kids, the work was less frustrating. I loved the years when my children were in school; I got a lot of pleasure out of them growing up."

BARRY, 66
investor, consultant, arts critic, retired manufacturer

"I was out of my first job at age twenty-four, when the company closed that facility. I was referred to another job in sales, nothing to do with my experience. I got the job, got introduced around to everyone by the person I was reporting to, and the next day he's gone. It was, There's your desk, there's the pile of stuff that's been sitting here for four weeks, it's yours, baby. I had to learn a whole new technology on the spot.

"A few years later, another big turning point. I had a wife, two kids, a lot of bills, and I'm being recruited for this job in electronics, which was completely esoteric to me although at the same time the field I had in mind back in high school. I took the chance. Took a couple of people from the old company with me, started the process of learning that business, and a few years after that we had half the market, tripled the business.

"I was director there until I retired myself at fifty-four, then got into arts criticism and business consulting. What I did for myself to plan a financially smart exit strategy I started doing for a bunch of other guys. I registered with the state, did it all legal, and I started managing money. I'm still doing it, but I might spend eighty hours one week, then nothing for two weeks."

THERESA, 58
retired management supervisor in an oil company

"From clerk I went into the accounting office, a lot of paperwork. Next, I got passed over for one position I really wanted in customer relations. Then I got a supervisor's position, managing field operations. In my final management job, I was kind of a one-person operation, with a male secretary. I loved that!

"I always stayed with the company, and I always felt lucky I could do that. I never went looking for something else. But I think if I had come into the company at a later point in time, I might have become a vice president. But they didn't make women vice presidents."

DAVE, 64
retired talent agent

"After the trade magazine and the technical manuals I worked for, I made a big change, age thirty-one. Joined a talent agency and had to start learning the whole framework of the motion picture business — how it worked, how scripts worked, how the hiring was done, a very complex and competitive business. I worked reasonably hard. I was well thought of.

"In my late thirties, an opportunity came along to develop a TV show based on a script that I had found. So I left the agency, which was actually a very clearly structured, service kind of business, and tried this whole new, entrepreneurial, free-form kind of work. Your day is yours to make of it what you will. In one way, nothing is expected of you, and in another way, everything is expected. I didn't have the motivation and confidence to operate out of structure. In three years I got one TV pilot made, which went nowhere.

"So I went back to the agency, eventually becoming a partner."

MAY, 84
psychologist in private practice

"I was a teaching assistant at a place I disliked and also working on my dissertation, at a snail's pace. An adviser of mine persuaded me I should join the army — this was the beginning of World War Two. So I joined, to my mother's horror.

"Midway through my four years there I got married. I was twenty-eight. After the war, we had three children in five years, then one more a few years later.

"I tried a full-time position, but it was impossible with the children still so young. So for about fifteen years I did a little of this and a little of that. I did testing for a pediatrician who ran a clinic, one day a week. More testing for one afternoon a week at the neuropsychiatric department in the local hospital.

"When my youngest was well launched in school, I went back to finish my degree. I was fifty-one when I got it, then did a seven-year postdoc, then spent a couple of years working for a medical director in a psychiatric unit. A great apprenticeship, doing some therapy before I really knew what the hell I was doing. And I've been in private practice ever since."

◆ ◆ ◆

From your bird's eye perspective of that span of job time, and your newly stirred-up memories of turning points and transitions, draw some conclusions about personal strengths and soft spots.

For example, you probably discovered aspects of work you took to with ease and others that were more of a struggle.

Ellen M., who's been a staff writer at three women's magazines, said that in some respects she was "a bad, bad fit" with her chosen career. She recalled a remark made by one of her editors-in-chief: "In the context of announcing who would be going to a sales conference in Florida, and I was not one of them, she said, 'Ellen's my backroom girl, I should get her one of those green eyeshades.' This comment both horrified me and infuriated me, briefly."

Thinking it over later, Ellen said, she became somewhat less horrified and infuriated. "At least she was smiling when she said it! But really, I knew what she meant, and she was right. Sitting at my desk, preferably with the door closed, I did terrific work, which she appreciated. On the other hand, at sales conferences, brainstorming sessions — at all that, I was usually dreadful. I am not a big 'thinking fast on your feet' type of person. I'm too self-conscious."

Larry L., a sales executive, knew what he was best at: "Lining up priorities in the midst of confusion, figuring out what was most critical in the long run, and taking action based on that." It's a skill at focusing that he traced back to the hectic years when he was a married father of four young children, employed full-time, and still working at completing a college degree: "There were always so many things that entered into the equation of why I'd rather not go to those night classes. I'd much rather stay home with the kids, shoot a little basketball, hang out with my wife. But I made school my primary goal for that point in time; I said, Come hell or high water I'm going to do it, and I'm going to avoid the temptations and obstacles. So that was a tremendous exercise in time management that I think has carried over into my business psyche or discipline."

Think now about four or five of your own happy or not

so happy work aspects, or the strengths that carried you along. For example:

- What, would you say now, was your strongest and most useful asset? (Going with the flow? Getting along with all kinds of people? Running with whatever ball was tossed to you?)
- Did you most enjoy novelty, variety, and ambiguity, or certainty, predictability, and the familiar?
- Have you always functioned most effectively or felt most energized as an individual, or as part of a team?
- Have you been a people person, or a paper person?
- Did you take easily to a new technology or a different way of doing things?
- Any mentors or role models who appeared along this part of your road?

As you note who impressed you and why, see if you can come up with at least one of the opposite sex. Many of us now in the forty-five-to-sixty-five age range, who lived through our earliest formative years before the feminist revolution radically altered cultural perceptions, were raised in a gender-specific fashion. Call to mind an opposite-sex individual, and give some thought to what it was about him or her you found admirable or powerful.

Head the next page in your notebook:

What I Loved, What I Hated; What I Was Good At, What I Was Not Good At

JACK, 58
school guidance counselor

"I'm pretty good at interacting with the students and with some of the other counselors and teachers. I like helping the kids with some of their personal problems. But I don't think I'm great at it, not like my supervisor when I first started at the school. She had a way of listening to the kids that was outstanding, always coming up with just the right question or comment geared to keep a kid talking or get him thinking. I was never that patient.

"More on the down side — I hate the paperwork, especially totally pointless reports. Can't stand gabby workshops that I have to attend. I have to deal with know-nothing administrators who are bossy and arbitrary, rules people. Plus some of the kids, not many, are fresh and unappreciative."

ISABELLA, 45
communications director for a medical equipment manufacturer

"I can articulate, in writing, rather difficult and boring facts about the business my company is in, and have them sound clear, concise, and even fascinating, if I'm on a roll. All those exercises in parsing and punctuation and spelling that got drilled into us in grammar school really taught me how to write well, which I've discovered very few people know how to do. But while I can admire myself for this, it isn't something I especially enjoy doing.

"What I hate, and have always hated, is sitting in an office all day — in my little suits and little silk shirts! I always admired the people who showed up for work looking like they really wanted to be there, as if the job was really important and they were really happy to be doing it."

MAX, 58
vice president with a food company

"Going back to my early days in TV production and, generally speaking, show business, to my surprise I didn't like the people I was meeting. I was both sort of intimidated and disgusted by them. They were driven, hustling, not nice people. You wanted to wipe your hand on your shirt after you shook hands. There was also a lot of shouting in the studios, people wanting to get their pound of flesh out of me, nobody saying thanks.

"During the same time, I was going to comedy-club open-mike nights — you paid the promoters a few bucks, and you could get up onstage and do your shtick. These were sleazy guys, and the audiences were usually worse, loud and rude. I had to work hard to get a few laughs. Some nights I didn't get any. So this was eye-opening time. Max the little comedian wasn't so funny after all.

"Giftwares, that whole business, was a con job. You were pitching these tchotchkes that were basically junky stuff nobody needed. Selling was not my forte. Neither was running restaurants, because that was all wrapped up with my personal going-back-to-the-nest issues, trying to settle some old scores, which I didn't pull off very well.

"Basically, I never followed through on anything until I got into my last, and current, job in food management. And there, as I've said, I've done pretty well, made money, got some family approval finally. Although I never thought I'd end up in business.

"Mainly, over the years, I haven't liked most of the people I thought I would like, and I've hated people telling me what to do."

SHEILA, 55
senior partner in a law firm

"I lucked into some decent jobs, but also I was good. I always had a lot of confidence, right from the start. And a lot of common sense, which I came to realize counts for as much as anything else.

"I'm good at getting to the essence of a problem, identifying the issue, and coming up with creative solutions. Another thing I'm good at, I think, is relating to people.

"What I like about my work now is coming and going pretty much as I please. What I haven't liked is doing the same thing over and over, getting to feel very familiar with a certain aspect of law and then not moving on, learning something new. And really, a bigger issue — I think now that it's a mistake to stay in the same field your whole adult life. It's too long.

"I loved especially getting to know a couple of lawyers I worked with off and on, a man and a woman — not because of anything they did in the legal field but because they had lives outside. One was an amateur painter; he did some good work and even exhibited and sold things. The other was painstakingly restoring an old house in the country. They always had an air about them of taking the law seriously, but not *that* seriously."

BARRY, 66
investor, consultant, arts critic, retired manufacturer

"What I've been good at, right from the start, is learning lessons from the negatives of life. Here's a story that goes back to when I was a kid having my Mr. Salty pretzel sticks and milk and listening to my radio shows. One evening, amazingly, we were out of pretzels. So I drank my milk, no pretzels, and when I woke up the next morning, for the first time in recorded history my mouth wasn't dry and parched. This was news! Waking up with your mouth all puckered isn't the normal state but is caused by pretzels! In other words, what one considers the natural condition of things may not be natural at all, but related to external, aberrant causes. That helped me the rest of my life. Whenever something seemed sort of off-kilter, I'd say, 'Is this natural or something aberrational that can be changed?'

"My best mentors were negative mentors. I learned from them how not to screw up in business. These guys, in several cases, were responsible for my moving on and taking some chances and relying on myself. Two examples. At the point I had to decide about jumping fields, I realized I already was better than my supervisor; he knew less than I did. So since he wasn't going anywhere, where could I go if I stayed? I left.

"There was another guy, a real hard worker from eight-thirty to five, and come five-oh-one, he was out the door. He also went nowhere. What I learned from him was that from eighty-thirty to five you earn your salary and that after five you earn your promotion or your success or your recognition. My whole work orientation changed.

"My strongest asset is this: I'm great at constructing my work around the specific skills that work for me. I work very hard to do the things I'm good at, and I shuck off the rest. The trick is to think in parts, see your personal organization chart as jigsaw pieces to move around.

"And right now, what I like best — I like being able to work at night by myself. I'm most creative at night."

THERESA, 58
retired management supervisor in an oil company

"I pride myself on the fact that I was both a good people person and a good paper person. When I was passed over for that first promotion, I learned a lot from my supervisor at the time. I went to her to complain, and she really turned my thinking around. She was kind of unattractive, not terribly well dressed, and sometimes very loud, and at the same time she was kind and caring to talk to. She explained the promotion situation to me in such a clarifying but soothing, supportive way, and I learned that the most important thing was to be fair to people. That became the guiding principle I operated by. If someone who's working for you isn't doing a good job, don't embarrass her in front of others, but be very clear about your expectations. And stick up for somebody if you think he's getting a raw deal.

"And then, I always wanted to understand what I was doing. When computers first came in, I asked how they worked and what you could do with them. There was one task I needed to do, and the computer expert said, 'If you think it up, we can program it.' That amazed me and inspired me. So I actually recommended a lot of changes over the years that were implemented. Some other people I worked with hated learning the computer. I didn't let it scare me."

DAVE, 64
retired talent agent

"At the service-oriented activities of my work life, I've been good. At the political or competitive aspects of the business, I have been reasonably lousy. Nevertheless, I at some point in the more recent years realized I was making it in this business, almost in spite of myself. I could figure out how to hire people, write checks, take nos, be in charge. I had brushes with fame, clients who did very well. The fact that I could make all that happen was quite remarkable to me.

"I have to say, though, that I was never as productive as I should have been, nor especially frugal. So in terms of what I was good at, what I was not so good at, I was good enough at the business, but I never really took the work seriously enough. I always had that notion that my work did not define me.

"But I behaved myself well in what is really a pretty rough business. I was always honest and honorable."

MAY, 84
psychologist in private practice

"Once I settled into my own practice, there was nothing I didn't like about the work. As I said at the start, listening to people and helping them figure themselves out is what I am ideally suited for — intellectually, temperamentally, socially.

"What I remember most over the years are the people I studied under, many of them powerful mentors, men and women. A lovely psych professor in college, an encouraging, warm woman. The professor who pushed me on for the Ph.D., he was great. Several more who always knew what I needed next, whom I should meet or study with.

"My ego ideal was a woman director of a clinic I worked in, a remarkable lady. A great deal more assertive than I ever was or have been, she assumed a leadership role in a natural, warm, but powerful way. I tried to model aspects of myself after her."

◆ ◆ ◆

He's worked for three architecture firms over the past twenty-three years, said Jay T., forty-eight, and at some point along the way he accepted that his original dream was probably unlikely to come to pass: "I always thought I'd have my own company someday, designing vacation homes or renovating the gorgeous, dilapidated old places in some of the small, semirural upstate towns that people are rediscovering. That was the initial goal." Reviewing his career path and strengths and soft spots, Jay thought he never had a sufficiently entrepreneurial spirit to pull that off. "I'm a perfectly competent architect," he said. "But I never really felt the fire in the belly to start my own business, when it came down to it."

He's not terribly unhappy about that, however: "The work we do is mainly store interiors, things of that nature, not too exciting," he said. "But it's a solid company; we keep generating a lot of business. Nobody ever has to be laid off."

Besides, he said, "I think I've come out with more goodies in some ways than I ever expected to have. For a long time, in my college and early working years, for example, I used to ride around the lake on my bike, thinking how I was really craving to live on that lake but not seeing how it would ever happen. And now, we've got our house on the lake. It's a great place for the kids. My wife and the kids and I go sailing eight months out of the year."

Recently he's started getting involved with his old high school again, first designing — at a fellow alumni's request — a new logo in celebration of the school's fiftieth year in existence. "I hadn't been in the place since I graduated," Jay said, "and it was a real charge, walking through it, seeing what had changed and what was absolutely the same as ever." He was charged enough to take part in running the anniversary festivities, and now he is heading up plans for the thirtieth reunion of his class: "I'm expecting that to be a hoot and a half, and also a good place to get people thinking about fund-raising. I want to see if we can drum up some money to hire a graphics instructor for a couple of years. Get some kids thinking about architecture. I'm having a lot of fun with this."

Jay's impressions typify a common state of mind that

settles on many individuals toward the end of their "coming to grips" years. He feels no particularly keen sense of disappointment or loss over the fading of an old job-related dream. As he's let that one go, he is able to consider the broad arc of his working life, and value the rewards of relative job security and a decent income in an iffy field.

Other life goals are increasing in importance for him now — the house on the lake, a dream that he did make happen; the time with family; volunteering. Jay recognized he had "shifted gears," he said, "rearranged my priorities. Or they rearranged themselves."

Looking at the view from what I call the great plateau, he was reassessing the situation — as you will do next.

CHAPTER 6

REFLECTING:
The View from the Great Plateau

fter the career-scrambling and family-building hurly-burly has largely settled down, life may assume a calmer and even more contented mien. Perhaps you find yourself now at midlife more satisfied with your work or career than at any previous time — you've discovered the right fit there; or you have enjoyed a high measure of success and feel pleasantly motivated but not excessively pressured to keep right on being successful; or you have accepted that this is as good as it gets, and that's all right with you. You have much company: between the ages of forty and sixty, concluded the MacArthur Foundation Research Network on Successful Midlife Development, the majority of American men and women report increased feelings of well-being and a greater sense of control over many parts of their lives. In general, they enjoy "psychic equanimity, good health, productive activity and community involvement."[13]

My experience as a therapist and interviews with scores of individuals for this book confirm another conclusion of that report, that the infamous "midlife crisis," a period of supposedly almost volcanic emotional pressures that lead to the throwing over of all former traces, doesn't happen to many people, and rarely so volcanically. At the same time, most of the men and women I have talked to found themselves becoming somewhat more reflective, more introspective, more interested in the broader picture of life and what they should make of it. They are often, too, evaluating their personal bits of unfinished business.

Certainly, passing what may be the midway mark can alter one's focus and produce some shifting of gears. Several researchers describe that shift in their study, "Taking Time Seriously": "When time is perceived as open-ended, knowledge-related goals are prioritized. In contrast, when time is perceived as limited, emotional goals assume primacy. . . . A more present-oriented state emerges, likely to involve goals related to feeling states, deriving emotional meaning and experiencing emotional satisfaction. . . . Relieved of concerns for the future, kindness becomes more prominent, and the search for existential meaning in life places emotion at the center stage."[14]

A retired cardiologist saw the shift this way: "For the first fifty years a man's life work is driven by hormones and biology. Over the next fifty years come goals derived from intellect and wisdom. So we have the maturation of enjoyment foci, from pure sex, liquor, tobacco, gambling, job hustling, and sports, to the pleasures of service, deepening marital intimacy, family support, the honing of private talents, friends, games, and simple fun."

Whether your own view from the great plateau has to do with more kindness and existential meaning, or with less smoking and drinking, or with something else entirely, indulge in some reflections now.

Consider, for one thing, your personal ideology or beliefs. By this time, your life is guided by principles and values as much as by wants and desires. You may not have articulated those guiding principles for yourself, but they exist. And at this stage of the game, you probably have a larger worldview than before.

Consider how you have combined work, family, and other interests, and whether shifts have been occurring lately in those realms.

Consider, perhaps, when you fit your own life best, when you felt most comfortable with who you were, or if the best, you hope, is still to come. Would you, right now, call yourself a success? Why?

◆ ◆ ◆

As you muse on these matters, you might find it useful to think of the balance you have struck among the requirements of your career, the time devoted to family needs and pleasures, and the concern you have devoted to other areas of personal interest and importance. Some questions that may be pertinent to your autobiography:

◆ Are you happy with the amount and kind of attention you gave to your children during the career-intense years? Is that a bit of "unfinished business" you'd like to redress?

Men, in particular, often enter a more nurturing phase about now and think they could have been better fathers in the past. One who is dippy about his two young grandchildren worries that he didn't achieve a great balance between career and family, a point his wife brought up: "She said, 'You really seem to be enjoying these kids,' referring to the grandchildren. 'It's a shame,' she said, 'you were never around to enjoy your own kids that way.' And that kind of put the knife through my heart, because I know it's true." However, although he always spent a lot of time at work, he said, he's satisfied that at least, "I never brought my work problems home with me. My private life was my private life, and work was work."

Another man felt fortunate in working close to home in the early years of raising a family: "I don't know if I'd get an A, but I think I did a pretty good job of balancing. I was fifteen minutes away from the office, so I could go to school events and all. The measurement I can apply is that I have excellent, close relationships with my two now adult children."

◆ Are you happy with the time and attention you have given to your partner? If you anticipate passing many more hours of the day with your partner in the future than you do now, is that prospect pleasant or somewhat alarming?

A woman who contemplates at least another seven or eight years at the job, married to a man who contemplates at least five or six more at his, looks at her older sister's experience as something of a cautionary tale. "My sister and her husband both quit working at about the same time," said Lydia R., a statistician. "Before that, he had his work, she had her work, they had each other. She had a lot of girl-friends, he didn't have a lot of guy friends.

"Now they're completely out of sync. She's got a lot going on, and there he is, and she doesn't know what to do with this little husband. So she's thrown herself into the role of being responsible for how he's doing — is he busy, is he happy? And she doesn't want that role, but she's right smack into it."

It reminded her, Lydia said, of their own mother, who had a hard time adjusting to her abruptly retired husband: "My father got very cranky and moody for a few years there. I think he just couldn't figure out how to redirect himself, and he was kind of hanging around her all the time. My mother was pulling out her hair. She used to say, 'I married him for better or worse but not for lunch.'"

The secret to contented coexistence, said a retired college professor, is "separate lives in the same house." She and her husband, also retired, are both "congenital over-achievers, but while I'm overachieving my stuff, he's over-achieving his stuff. We can exist very comfortably for hours doing our own things in the same house. In the same room, in fact — he's at his laptop at one end of this fifteen-foot-long old refectory table we have in the dining room, and I'm with my laptop at the other." Every so often they take a break for coffee or a walk together.

◆ Is something about the world at large getting your juices flowing these days? Do you recognize in yourself a redirected focus, a diminishing of self- and family absorption, a wish to give back after years of taking in?

Maybe politics, polluted lakes, homophobia, overpopulation, or civil wars are bothering you deeply, although you hadn't given much thought to such matters before. Maybe you're starting to wonder what you can do about them. A horticulturist said that more and more he felt "a growing feeling of disgust about the excesses of our society, a place where some people apparently are willing to pay twenty thousand dollars for a wristwatch. Dismay at the lack of civility and people's feelings of entitlement, like it's an outrage that there aren't more checkers at the upscale take-out food store and you have to stand on line for three minutes." He was wondering, he said, about his "moral imperatives, what if anything I can do to promote what I consider responsible, generous, decent ways of living."

Give all this some thought, and write your impressions on the next page of your notebook:

THE BALANCING ACT: MY WORK, MY FAMILY, AND THE REST

JACK, 58
school guidance counselor

"I was ninety percent work, maybe more, ten percent wife and kids. This is something I feel bad about. I'm not real close to my kids these days. It's funny — with the students at school, I was always sympathetic and helpful, and with my own boys, I was pretty strict and bossy. I thought that's what a father should be.

"I did have a lot of time off the job, because of the summer vacations, but I worked other jobs or did repair work on the house, not much of anything else. So it's never been a great balance, you'd say.

"If my wife and I both stop working about the same time, I don't know how great that's going to be, to tell you the truth. Mostly we talk about our jobs and the kids. I'm going to need something else."

ISABELLA, 45
*communications director for a medical
equipment manufacturer*

"The balance of my time went into the jobs I've had. The balance of my emotions went elsewhere—my family, my friends, my social life, various hobbies or things I like doing. It seems to me kind of a shame to spend so much of your waking hours doing something that doesn't actually mean a whole lot to you. But I have a full life in other ways.

"Actually, I do feel at a plateau right now. Not having kids makes you start thinking about what you're going to leave behind, not to get too corny about it. I want to start casting around for new involvements, maybe do some charity work."

MAX, 58
vice president with a food company

Despite his sometimes turbulent marital life, Max was a great dad, he thought, when his two daughters were little: "I was the pied piper. I'd go to the playground with the girls, and in ten minutes I had a pack of little kids trailing after me. I could be a clown with little kids, telling them jokes, playing goofy games. My girls used to throw their arms around me and say, '*My* daddy!' They were always all over me as soon as I got home. After my divorce, when they lived with their mom and were getting into the teenage years, I didn't have so much input anymore.

"But the big shifting gears came at one point when I decided to find out more about myself, what was motivating me, and I got very heavily into therapy workshops, EST groups, all that touchy-feely stuff. I even began training to become a lay psychoanalyst, but I didn't really have the time or the motivation. But it was good, in that I stopped looking at what's wrong with all the other guys who were giving me a hard time and started looking at what's wrong with me. It sort of explained the comedy and the performing as a way of getting the love and attention I didn't get elsewhere.

"Overall, I've probably been a better vice president than a father, maybe than a husband, too. What I needed to do at work was clear to me. What I needed to do at home was less clear — in fact, a big muddle a lot of the time. Lately that's been less true. Whatever comes next, it's got to involve my wife and family."

SHEILA, 55
senior partner in a law firm

"When my kids were little, I thought that part of life was great. I was younger and I had more energy, more enthusiasm, and I did love being a mother. However, I would have to say I didn't do a spectacularly good job at balancing the various aspects of my life. The proof now is in the pudding — I never developed any real hobbies, never pursued activities other than work and raising kids.

"I don't blame myself for that especially, because I was incredibly busy doing just those two things for twenty or so years. Now that my family role is a very small part of my life, with the kids no longer here and no grandchildren, there's only the work.

"But more and more these days, I'm appalled and revolted by so much of what I read and learn in the news. The United Nations Human Development Report this year made me despair about this world. There are about four and a half billion people in developing countries, and a third of them don't have clean water to drink. A fifth of them have no modern health services at all. Thinking about these things weighs on me; it seems to pull me back to the old dream of making a real difference, and the fact that I didn't do anything close to that."

BARRY, 66
investor, consultant, arts critic, retired manufacturer

He saw the central arc of his career-building time, a stretch of about twenty-five years, "as an intensely volatile period," Barry said. "I wasn't keeping things on an even keel at times — emotionally distracted in my personal life, in an unwise relationship that took more mental energy to handle than the immature person I was had. I plowed myself then entirely into the work, to the detriment of other aspects of life."

The balance is better now, he thought, "because I have the insight and the ability to manage it better. Three things are important to me — work, marriage, kids. The work tends to be the most successful, maybe unfortunately, but I want to have all three going on concurrently, to some measure happily. I like to be multifunctional in multiple areas. And try to be a better grandparent than I was a parent."

He's proud of his avocation, arts criticism, and the involvements that brought that about and still are a significant part of his life: "I was on the chamber of commerce, this is fifteen or so years ago, and I wanted to create a broader culture in the city, so I arranged some fund-raisers, got all the execs to come, and we got a repertory theater started. There's a huge amount of regional stuff going on these days — small jazz groups, dance performances. I think I'm disseminating some of that influence by trekking around to these venues, writing about that kind of creative energy."

THERESA, 58
retired management supervisor in an oil company

"I was a good daughter, even though I felt pulled a lot of the time for years when my mother lived in a nursing home, because I was the only one around to see to her needs. But I did it. And I'm a good wife.

"I've always been involved in my church, helping run dinner dances to raise money for the poor. So that's rewarding.

"But the day-to-day balance was a lot more satisfying when I was working. All the things I do around the house now, the cleaning and shopping and cooking, I used to do then, too, but now they can take the whole day. It's as though the chores expanded to fill the time. I just used to feel so competent to be a full-time worker and a full-time wife and housekeeper."

DAVE, 64
retired talent agent

"I'd say my life has been excellently balanced all along. My mantra was always, Work is not the center of my life. I do it because I have to and I'm good at it, but living it is another thing. I was always thinking my real life was outside the job — travel, the arts, theater, film, family. In my own mind I was a Renaissance, creative guy who just happened to be an agent. The agent part was kind of an act.

"So I was never the stereotypical workaholic husband and father. We had a great time for years, still do — an awful lot of friends, an enormous and complex social life, traveling to some really fabulous places. And I've always talked to my kids a lot; I tried to share with them the mistakes I made and give them some ideas of how to avoid them. They grew up wonderfully well, and I give my wife and myself some credit for that.

"But what started to come to the fore, right about the time I left work, was this — I wanted to find out who I am as a person, minus the framework of business. I am not Dave the agent, but Dave . . . what? That was, in a sense, a missing piece of the picture, and one I have been giving an excess of thought to, and not coming up with clear answers."

MAY, 84
psychologist in private practice

"Overall my work and family balance was good. There were many years when the family had to come first, so I gave them that time. It's the central problem for every woman, how to live on both sides. And it's not an easy one to solve. But I think I did solve it well. When the family needed me less, the work took me over more."

◆ ◆ ◆

When Valerie G., age forty-six, decided three years ago to leave her job as assistant director of the music department in a school for adult continuing studies, she had a goal: "I wanted to combine my two loves, music and travel, and have more time with my family and friends. Now I give private guitar and piano lessons in my apartment, fixing my own schedule. I might go for several months seeing fifteen students a day and knocking myself out, then I take off — last year, I spent the winter holidays in London with my sister, a month in Greece with my boyfriend, and a month in Tuscany with my other sister and some friends."

At this point in her life, she said, she considers herself "definitely a success. I end up the year with astonishingly little money considering what I charge per hour and how many hours I teach. But I've elected to spend my money and a lot of time with the people and in the places that I love. It's the right trade-off."

For other individuals, "success" was strongly colored by whether they ended their run on the career path in the place they wanted to be. Harry L. calls himself "only mildly successful," although he's an enormously well paid top manager in a *Fortune* 500 company and a contented family man. Harry kept resetting his goals, he said, always pushing the next one a little higher but still, he thought, within reach: "I never really wanted to get in a comfortable corner. Sit back and say, Phew, I made it." Now he considers himself not a real success because "I'm not going to retire as chairman of the board."

Viewing matters now from the great plateau, analyze your own definition of success, and whether you have achieved it.

- ◆ Do you equate it with personal mastery, earning power, making a useful contribution, or some combination of those?
- ◆ Or with "the right trade-off," perhaps in terms of achieving a gratifying mix of work, family, and "other"?
- ◆ Has your feeling of success come about partly or largely in comparison with others?

It's generally understood that individuals' level of aspiration, or the height at which they set their goals and the kind of performance they expect of themselves, is significantly influenced by group standards. We may raise or lower our goals, in other words, and expect more or less of ourselves, according to the company we keep.

- ◆ If, looking back over your career path, you decide you were not much of a success at all, or even something of a flop, to what do you attribute that conclusion?

Perhaps, like Harry, whom most would consider a successful businessman, you have been reaching for the unreachable star, and you are doing a number on yourself based on those idealized goals. It's helpful to recognize such tendencies now, because bringing goals into the doable range will be critical to your future feelings of achievement and satisfaction.

But if you think you really should or could have gone a lot further than you did, do you chalk up your less-than-stellar accomplishments to your own shortcomings (you weren't smart enough, you didn't try hard enough) or to the influences of others ("they" were out to get you, the breaks never came your way, it was fate)? Again, it will be useful to run a little reality check, to consider as objectively as possible the relative effects of internal and external causes, and to "own" your part in what didn't work. Then, as you continue to figure out what you're going to do when you grow up, you will be in a good position to think about what you might do differently on that next go-around.

Jot down your thoughts on a new page. Call it:

MY SUCCESS EQUATION

JACK, 58
school guidance counselor

"I keep harking back to when I went after a principal's job and kind of chickened out. I guess I never had been the decision maker before, or the place where the buck stopped. And I was afraid to be that. So that's a sense of disappointment in myself.

"But I kept my job, got my raises. And the most satisfying thing was seeing a youngster get his act together as a result of something I did. I did that for a lot of kids, and that was worth more than money. That was my success."

ISABELLA, 45
*communications director for a medical
equipment manufacturer*

"I was always smarter than practically everybody else in school, right through college, which made me feel good. I had my working in and bumming around Europe spell, which also made me feel good about myself.

"After that, success as a smart, adventurous, creative individual carving out a work life that utilizes her full potential? No."

MAX, 58
vice president with a food company

"Being a success, in my book, means growing up. It means you feel like a full-fledged adult. You know what you want, you know what you don't want. You know how to get what you want. I know a few people I consider really successful, and they're not necessarily the guys or the gals who've made a lot of money or have the title or the prestige or whatever. These people radiate a kind of calm, serene manner. They have that aura about them, like they've *arrived* wherever they should be, and some of them didn't have all happy, trouble-free lives by any means.

"So no, I'm no big success in my life so far."

SHEILA, 55
senior partner in a law firm

"I was successful in high school. I was almost always happy. That was a good, fun time. But it's a little harsh and depressing to think you capped your career back in high school!

"Overall, I don't feel like a huge success, I'd have to say. I can congratulate myself on being a good mother, which I was and am, and on being a good lawyer. But I measure success by happiness. Not money or prestige or status, because I have a good measure of that. But really, happiness in your day-to-day life, and I'm not happy a lot of the time. There are too many days that I'm not feeling any joy or pleasure, or I feel just flat at work."

BARRY, 66
investor, consultant, arts critic, retired manufacturer

"I've been fantastically successful in business, and moderately successful but getting better in the private sphere, so no complaints."

THERESA, 58
retired management supervisor in an oil company

"Success is how you come out of it, how you live your life. Do you live it looking back and saying, I should have done things in a different way, or do you live it saying, I did the best I could? And I do look back and think that's what I did.

"I still think I could have made vice president. But I

have no bad feelings about that in a personal way, because there's nothing I could have done differently. I guess I just wish that I could accept my life now better than I do. Accept the things that can't be changed, like not being able to have the kind of interaction with people I had on the job."

DAVE, 64
retired talent agent

"Well, some things didn't turn out the way I thought they would turn out. I changed careers a couple of times and never did just what I wanted to do, and then, I was neither terribly productive nor terribly frugal and I ended up with less money than almost everyone I know. And now, I still beat myself up over those questions: Why didn't I do better? What was wrong with me that here, relatively late in life, I'm saying, Well, if we do this, we can't afford to do that? And were my parents right after all, that I was always too much of a daydreamer to make a good living? So when I measure success that way, I feel like a failure. I do myself in, in a lot of ways.

"Then, my plan for this wonderful retirement pretty much fizzled. I truly believed that this was going to be my coming-into-my-own time, when I was going to be the most content with myself and my life, and I haven't been able to pull that off.

"However, if I can get past those things in my mind, I do feel like a success. My blessings are enormous. I love my wife, my wife loves me. Nothing terrible has happened in my life, I'm healthy, everyone is fine, no tragedies."

MAY, 84
psychologist in private practice

"I measure success by the feedback I get from my patients, and it is consistent and good. I regularly hear out of the blue from people I haven't treated or seen in years, and they tell me how helpful I've been to them or their kids and so on — warm and fuzzy stuff.

"When in my life have I been most comfortable with who I am? Probably now. It's an interesting subject, elderly people who sustain their careers, because the competition is ferocious. But I'm competing still, and that's surely a success."

◆ ◆ ◆

Take a breather from reflecting.

That little spiral-bound notebook by now is no doubt filled with a variety of intriguing bits and pieces, from how you once wanted to be a tightrope walker in the circus, to why you hated your first boss, to what you think about having grandchildren. In the next chapter, we pull together the bits and pieces, to take a look at the picture they form: first, what interests, talents, dreams, or needs are most likely to lead you toward a genuinely rich and flourishing life after work, and second, what in your makeup will propel you forward or might hold you back.

CHAPTER 7

WHAT I WANT TO DO WHEN I GROW UP:
A Plan for the Rest of the Story

T hose jottings in your notepad constitute a thumbnail sketch of the prevailing currents in your autobiography so far. Let us discern now the pattern they make and the message they send about what you might (probably) do with (at least part of) the rest of your life. Then we'll see how you'll do it, considering in particular the changes, if any, that are in your own best interest — why and where you might need to move yourself a bit out of character, for example, in order to move on.

To start, go back to the second page in your notebook, "Fifteen Good Things (Besides Money) I Get from My Job." Look over that list and check off the four or five that, with perhaps now heightened awareness, you realize are most important for you. Whatever your next life moves, if you don't find a way to replace, replicate, or incorporate these items, you're going to feel more at sea than you want to be.

After that thoughtful look, read through the rest of your story. Linger and ponder a bit over any realizations, memories, people, or turning points that strike you now as particularly significant or surprising, energizing or rueful and that seem to send a siren call or a red-flag warning.

When you have completed your review, give it a little time to sink in.

Sleep on it.

Then do this final bit of homework, your personal Twenty Questions inventory.

Psychologists for decades have offered various versions of the following categories and various definitions for them — a life-goals inventory, a self-assessment profile, a self-concept test. Perhaps in the distant past, at a time you were trying to come up with a suitable career to pursue, you wandered into your college's guidance office and completed one of those questionnaires — on which you indicated you strongly liked or strongly disliked the thought of being a brain surgeon or a bush pilot, or decided you valued sentiment more than logic, or checked off everything that applied to you on a list of three hundred adjectives, from "absent-minded" to "zany." Perhaps you came away at the end with a genuinely useful suggestion. On the other hand, you may have wondered what that was all about, as did a computer technician I talked to whose profile decreed his ideal job was shepherd.

I have invented my own version of a self-profile, evolving closely from the various questions you have been answering in your notebook and from my interpretations of what you need to know to keep growing up: the ten motivators and the ten activators.

What I Want, What I Need: The Ten Motivators

Within each of these general categories fall the individual and unique needs, wants, interests, and values that spark you, that have shaped much of your life so far, or that you realize with regret have been missing from your life. In one form or another, they will drive you forward, and from some combination of them you would be wise to devise a game plan for the future, because that combination is most likely to provide you with the greatest well-being in retirement. As we know now, well-being requires having meaning, establishing objectives, realizing potential, being open to new experiences, and finding the right fit. It means evolving in ways that reflect greater self-knowledge and effectiveness.

Coming up next are several questions or statements. Read them and plug in the conclusions you have reached about yourself.

The motivators:

1. Identity

Complete the phrase: "I am a _____."

You might want to consider this matter of "identity" in terms of the roles you play in your life, or the several hats you wear or have worn over the years. Pick your five prevailing roles — perhaps wife, mother, journalist, friend, craftsperson — and give them some thought. At this stage of the game, which would be the easiest to eliminate, the role you'd be most comfortable doing without? And the second? And third? What do you end up with?

The point is this: identity is a powerful component in self-image. If your work role is the one you would let go of last or most regretfully, your highest self-value and the way in which you are most likely to describe or "name" yourself, it will continue in some aspect to define who you are and how you think about yourself in your life after the job — perhaps to an uncomfortable degree. If journalist is your number one role, it might be wise now to begin focusing more intently on the others, against the day no one is paying you to write any longer.

The more ways by which you can identify yourself, in fact, the broader your vistas. In his book *The Virtues of Aging,* Jimmy Carter "names" himself thusly: "At different times in my life I have introduced myself as a submariner, farmer, warehouseman, state senator, governor, or even president, if that was necessary. I might have added where I lived, but that was about it. Now, even though not holding a steady job, I could reply . . . that I am a professor, author, fly fisherman, or woodworker. I could add American, southerner, Christian, married, or grandfather." Keeping a variety of identities and options going, he writes, "is a good indication of the vitality of our existence."[15]

2. Intellectual Activity
Have I sought out, required, and found great pleasure in intellectual stimulation?

If mental pursuits have always been or once were a wellspring of engagement, relaxation, or positive feedback — or the highlight of your job, the aspect you were best at and liked the most — you'll clearly need to find ways to keep on using your good brain. At least some component of your future activities will have to exercise your mental strengths, or you'll bore yourself.

3. Physical Activity

Has regular physical activity been an agreeable part of my life, in the past or at present?

If your answer is yes, then sports, exercise, working with your hands, or other physical pursuits should obviously be an agreeable part of your next act as well, probably an even greater part as you enjoy greater free time.

If your answer is "no, but I want to get more active because I know it's good for me" — the voice of an outside "should" — you'll do best to be conservative in your expectations. The guy who has never played much tennis in his life will not suddenly have gorgeous ground strokes.

4. Spiritual Attention

Is it important to me that I focus on the spiritual aspect of my life?

If the special qualities of some of your most unforgettable people centered on religious commitments, for example, or you feel a youthful interest in religion that you abandoned might be worth reinvestigating, attending to the spiritual side of your life may be a powerful motivator in what comes next.

Or perhaps you have no particular urge toward religion as such but rather experience the spiritual sense that life is good, that you have had more than a fair share of its bounty, and that now helping and being useful to others — making the world a better place — will be critical to your sense of well-being.

5. Friendships

Have I always sought out the company of friends, and missed it when I didn't have it?

If your human need for congenial social contact is great *and* has been gratified almost exclusively by your on-the-job friendships and connections, prepare to put a determined effort into establishing new ways to make those contacts.

On the other hand, maybe peaceful days at last with nobody much around and the greater freedom for solitary pursuits will satisfy your loner instinct and need.

6. Family Attachments

Do I derive a great deal of satisfaction from my family?

Maybe you have always relished being with your kinfolk and rued the reality of not having enough time to spend with them. Family enjoyment, then, or mending some relationship fences, is clearly a significant motivator for your after-the-job life.

Perhaps family relationships haven't especially been much fun or made you happy, and you see no reason to anticipate improvement on that score. That's okay; it's good to know ahead of time that filling the days to come with relatives will not be enough to satisfy you.

7. Applause and Recognition

Do I need external rewards?

Have you, for example, always tended to measure yourself against others to feel good about your accomplishments? The need to compete, to be recognized, or to win is a powerful motivator. If it's one of yours, you will be happiest finding at least one new outlet for that competitive drive.

8. Generative Efforts

Is it important to me that I pass on my knowledge, experience, skills, and talents?

Perhaps you found great pleasure, satisfaction, and

feelings of worth in training or teaching others in the things you were good at or cared about. "Showing the ropes" to the next generation or volunteering your expertise in civic and community activities should continue to be a purposeful aim, once you find a way to do it.

Or think of generative activities in the sense of producing or originating — as the personal expression of what you feel and all you've learned, through painting, writing, playing music, or other creative avenues. Is that a motivating need?

9. Activity Comfort Level

On a scale of 1 to 10, with 1 a couch potato and 10 a whirling dervish, where does it seem I am most comfortable?

The closer you have always been to the whirling-dervish end — the more comfortable you have always felt with lots of things to do — the easier it will be to get yourself moving in the open-ended days ahead. If a slow, quiet pace best suits your nature, you might relish the lack of to-do lists in the future, and feel no need to "keep busy."

However, the whirling dervish who hurls himself or herself into a flurry of activity and the couch potato who luxuriates in relative inactivity might each start to feel more enervated than invigorated — if each hasn't figured out some truly purposeful actions.

10. Risk Comfort Level

On a scale of 1 to 10, with 1 same old/same old and 10 skydiving, where am I most comfortable?

Over the years how great a degree of risk have you tolerated? And how happily or unhappily? Because you are about to invent a brand-new and significant portion of your life, taking chances will be necessary, and some element of risk goes along with that.

If you are a sky diver who always got a charge from adventure, tackling the new and different, you won't let it throw you off course. If you have always played it safe, however, new ventures may pose problems.

How I'll Get There, What Might Stop Me: The Ten Activators

Whatever your defined wants and needs, we can confidently predict that they will be influenced by some, most, or all of the following actions, tendencies, or effects: the activators.

Some, most, or all have been called for throughout your career-building years, too, although on the job your level of aspiration, motivation, and achievement needs have been at least partially shaped by external factors. Now, in the delightful period of life in which your time and energies will be yours to spend as you see fit, the boundaries and the impetus are up to you.

Based on what you have gleaned from your autobiography so far, decide whether you might reasonably and sensibly anticipate that each of the following activators will be either a strong suit or a roadblock in your progress. The strong suits, generally speaking, are those qualities that have always served you well and will probably continue to do so — perhaps you're good at switching gears when matters aren't working out very well, or you're a self-starter. Give yourself a pat on the back and rely on what you have going for you.

Pay attention as well to the roadblocks, what might at this point in your new, venturing-forth part of life tend to slow you down. These qualities are not necessarily bad. Just recognize them, accept them, and work with them or around them. At the very least, naming your roadblocks ensures that they won't blindside you.

The activators:

1. Making Choices

STRONG SUIT: *I'm good at figuring out for myself what I want to do.*

ROADBLOCK: *I haven't had much practice at making my own choices.*

Remembering those forks in the road, from the time you picked a college or opted for a particular career, consider whether it's your nature to listen to your own voice or to follow someone or something else's. More than ever now, your own voice is the one to heed, so if you have never made many choices over the years, that's a muscle to strengthen.

Or circumvent this roadblock by doing what makes you comfortable; ask others to help you figure out solid choices.

2. Initiating Action

STRONG SUIT: *I'm a self-starter.*

ROADBLOCK: *I need a push.*

Are you happiest following an imposed schedule? Does a stretch of unplanned time cause anxiety, or is it a vista of enticing possibilities?

Self-starters have no problems.

But if you have good ideas in mind, yet keep putting things off or don't know where to begin, try to find a like-

motivated companion to get you going. Or you may need
to push *yourself* more, by creating and adhering to a self-
imposed structure, shaping your days by giving yourself
assignments.

3. Setting Reasonable Goals

STRONG SUIT: *I usually set goals that are within reach,
maybe just a little higher than I'm absolutely certain I
can attain.*

ROADBLOCK: *I tend to set my sights on goals that are so
high that they discourage me or on goals that are too easy.*

Goals that are too low and easily achieved, we know,
don't lead to feelings of satisfaction, but ones that are essentially impossible dreams can cause frustration. If you
have always been at the high end of the spectrum, adjustments may be needed as you go about coming up with a
non-job-related set of goals. Maybe one of your major payoffs throughout your working years has been being the
best and the brightest at what you do, not just good
enough but outstandingly successful. It's in your bones,
then, to continue to expect to be outstandingly successful.
So recognizing that you will only and forever be just a
good-enough amateur classical guitarist may be a hard nut
for you to swallow, one that might tempt you to stop practicing your plucking. And that would be a shame.

Indeed, tinkering with the setting of personal goals
can be an invaluable adaptive skill to develop if you hope
to keep on growing up and feeling content well into old
age. That sense of well-being comes about, say psychologists, when older people "revise their goals to reflect possibilities and limitations for achievement and maintenance."
Aiming for a level of "*just manageable difficulty,* the point at

which they feel challenged given their current competencies and resources," produces the happiest outcome.[16]

In the next chapter, we take a closer look at this all-important business of goal setting, and the need you may have to set your sights a bit lower.

4. Proceeding Independently

STRONG SUIT: *I can happily go it alone when I have to.*

ROADBLOCK: *I need people around to give me feedback.*

In retirement, more than at any past point, you will be left to your own devices; you may find yourself keeping your own company much of the time. Thus, the ability to go it alone will be helpful.

But if some of your significant plans involve essentially solitary pursuits, and you are an individual who has always been most productive or felt most activated when bouncing ideas and energy off others, some adjustments may be called for. Devoting yourself to an intensive study of ancient Mayan cultures might be a lot more fun if you can hunt up a mentor to advise you, or two or three other enthusiasts to meet for talks or museum visits.

Besides, what you might put off doing on your own — an exercise routine, for example — you may embrace more willingly in the company of others or at a friend's behest.

5. Overcoming Obstacles

STRONG SUIT: *I've seen them, and in general, I've been able to get past the ones that are passable.*

ROADBLOCK: *I let them stop me.*

If in reviewing your autobiography you came away with a feeling of some dismay, sensing that too often you gave up when something difficult loomed before you, think a bit further about this matter of overcoming obstacles. Maybe you're being too hard on yourself, focusing exclusively on the times you've been stymied. Perhaps you were right to give up, because the obstacle was genuinely insurmountable (you wished to be a ballerina, but you tend to fall over your own feet). Perhaps an obstacle that was once powerful (the internalized voice of a critical parent) need no longer apply.

At the same time, everyone has had to get over some tough hurdles in life, including you. Conjure up one of yours, consider what you did right then and how you did it, and make that your mind-set and your encouragement.

6. Changing Course
STRONG SUIT: *I'm good at switching gears when something's clearly not working.*

ROADBLOCK: *When something's not working, I keep hammering away, trying to pound a square peg into a round hole.*

In the period of life you're about to enter, you'll be open to any number of possibilities. Some that sounded good at the start may bomb or turn out to be less satisfying than you had hoped. The ability to change course and try something new is one to cultivate.

Hanging in there can sometimes amount to dogged persistence that gets you nowhere. It really is acceptable to recognize when something isn't working, and that it's not necessarily because you're not trying hard enough, and to move on.

7. Striking a Balance
STRONG SUIT: *I'm satisfied overall with the balances and trade-offs I've made between work and play, personal needs and outside commitments.*

ROADBLOCK: *I get overly involved with one pursuit or area of life, to the neglect of others.*

If in evaluating your success equations you decided you'd been pretty good at striking a healthful and suitable balance in life — working and socializing, work and family roles, solitary activities and communal efforts, or whatever the combination you valued — you'll probably find it not terribly difficult to achieve a similarly comfortable mix once the job aspect is gone or greatly diminished.

On the other hand, maybe you've always been an individual of intensely single focus, and in the future you'd really like to loosen up and spread your energies and attentions across more varied aspects of life. This is a roadblock to chip away at; see how people you admire manage to strike a better balance.

However, if you are a single-focus, intense individual and have no desire to be any other way, forget about achieving some notion of the ideally balanced life, which after all isn't for everyone.

8. Following Through

STRONG SUIT: *I'm a finisher.*

ROADBLOCK: *I start off with a bang, then let things drift or peter out.*

Because the high-investment activities that lead to well-being call for a hefty degree of commitment and effort, stick-to-itiveness is clearly a strength that will serve you well.

However, since you have infinitely more latitude in retirement than you ever did on the job, where following through was both expected and demanded, your dog-with-a-bone tendencies might occasionally be relaxed. Or your inclination to drift will be more acceptable. Usually you can put off tomorrow or next month what you didn't get to today. Nobody will call you a slacker.

9. Experiencing a Sense of Achievement

STRONG SUIT: *When I've finished something, I enjoy the achievement and move on.*

ROADBLOCK: *I'm never quite satisfied with what I've done.*

If, based on your autobiography so far, you check this one off as a roadblock, perhaps there's been real cause for you to feel dissatisfied with aspects of your past progression through life. But if from here on in you are able to make personally meaningful choices, set reasonable goals, and take action, deem your efforts well and good and resolve to tell yourself that you have indeed achieved something.

10. Finding Pleasure

STRONG SUIT: *I value pleasure and allow myself to seek it.*

ROADBLOCK: *I feel guilty when I'm having too much fun.*

Lose the guilt. You've worked for years! Whatever you're going to do when you grow up, those pursuits should be, above all, pleasurable. And fun.

◆　◆　◆

Our eight friends, whose autobiographies you have been following as you've sketched out your own, went through the Twenty Questions inventory with me. Afterward, each reexamined his or her original retirement dreams, to consider whether what had come to mind then still seemed like a good idea — and whether new possibilities had appeared. And later still, three or four got some new plans under way.

Review their stories with me now, to see what we know about their growing up. Then try to review your own story in a similar manner.

JACK, 58
school guidance counselor

After listing his various roles (husband, father, son, brother, guidance counselor, educator), Jack thought for a while and then said: "I'd give up the son and brother roles first, then the guidance counselor." Jack clearly gets much emotional sustenance from his job — "good friends" and "people to talk to" were among his most valued positive payoffs there, and when he goes to work he feels he's "being good," he doesn't "act like a dope." But although work is of paramount importance to Jack, he gives it up as a significant role once he first lets go of the "son" role that pounded home the work ethic in his youth.

Jack then identified himself first and foremost as "an educator," which ties in directly with his number one payoff from the job — the occasional opportunity to help a troubled youngster. He won't mourn the end of his counseling career as long as he can find ways to sustain his identity as an educator.

With lengthy summer vacations and school holidays, Jack has had more than the typical amount of nonjob time. He's occupied himself during those times, however, largely with other kinds of work. A physically robust and active man, when he's not at the school Jack is busy with house repairs, for himself and his relatives; summers, he often works part-time construction jobs. Feeling guilty about having fun has always been a bugaboo for Jack. In his family, pleasure had a low priority — now, Jack hardly knows how to think about it. And this is a man who's worked steadily from the age of seven.

But he does vividly remember the great joy he found in playing stickball and baseball as a kid, riding a bike "to the farthest end of my tether, seeing how far I could get and then going a little farther." Those activities were not only fun, they incorporated a somewhat heroic quality; and Jack clearly liked the idea of being a hero, testing himself, "being cheered by the crowd." He has let all physical playtime go by the board since high school, however.

In his autobiography under "The Balancing Act," Jack had marked himself as 90 percent work, 10 percent family, and now, like many men, he looks back with some regret, fearing that he sounded with his children too much like his own father, the "bossy dictator." He's good with kids on the job, however; again, Jack's primary measure of success, where his pride lies, has been "seeing a youngster get his act together as a result of something I did."

Jack couldn't decide how to qualify his activity level, but I'd put him way up around 10. This is a man who clearly keeps going from the time he gets up in the morning until night. His risk comfort level, however, is low. Although he's responsible, throughout his job years he has never pushed the envelope very far. Still, he has a yen to do a little adventuring and be "less sheltered"; his educational road not taken was studying "something about international issues, world geography, economics maybe," and he greatly admired his world-traveling uncle Ed.

In his recollections of how he picked a college ("the closest one"), an area of study ("the ed courses didn't seem too difficult"), and an eventual career ("pretty much fell into it"), there's little indication of active choice on Jack's part. Being asked to think about what he wants is new for him. As he goes about making choices and initiating action, Jack would do well to share his thoughts with his wife or his favorite brother, someone who can help him talk things through and offer that bit of a push. He's not great at changing course, but he did it once: a significant turning point on his "Careers" map marked the time he left the school system voluntarily to take a corporate job. It was not to his liking, and he returned to the school. But Jack can look back now and give himself some encouraging words: "I made, for me, a radical move then, and the world didn't collapse."

Although his fear of "being the guy in charge" prevented him, he thinks, from moving up the career ladder to a principal's appointment, he is likely to feel more confident once he's free of official responsibilities. Recognizing that he missed an opportunity because of his fear gives him the chance to reflect on what there is to be afraid of now. Although he thinks he might have set his career goals a bit higher, Jack feels he has accomplished a lot; it's been a job well done. "I was never money driven. Even thinking about retirement, I don't need a lot of money." His measures of success and sense of achievement are available to him after he leaves the job.

And he's a finisher. Once he finds the right choices and initiates action, he will stick with it and follow through.

How Jack Reviewed His Retirement Dreams

When Jack took another look at his plans for the future, they seemed to come up woefully short — even to him, never much of a dreamer. But he was able to identify some needs and wants: "I like to be busy, I like being around people, I like feeling helpful." He recognized, too, that he'd be best doing things independently within structured situations, that he wanted to experience life on a bit broader stage, and that he wanted to get more of that playtime — "not fill up every day with just more kinds of work."

"I'm not a big self-starter, socially speaking," Jack said. His friends were all colleagues at work, and he sensed he'd lose touch with them once he retired; other social activities were arranged mostly by his wife, with Jack going along. He was a little nervous, too, when he contemplated the day both he and she will no longer be going to jobs: "Have to get some new things to talk about, or do. Get away from the house more, maybe." He resolved now to find a sport, perhaps racquetball, that he could participate in with others, and thought sports might even be a way to spend some quality, though not overly emotional, time with his adult sons, with whom he'd like to have a closer relationship. What really perked his interest was reading an article about slow-pitch senior softball and discovering that there was a league in a nearby town: "I never even heard of this before. Maybe it's something I could really do."

Other fresh ideas: Jack hadn't indulged his love of stamps since he was ten, an interest to take off the back burner: "I probably still have my old albums around. Lots of stamps since I stopped collecting!" He was going to see if he might coach Little League ("baseball and kids, a perfect combination for me"). And he planned to check into a travel agency for some brochures and information. But acknowledging that he is not much of a risk taker, he's thinking conservatively about his seeing-the-world plans: "The idea of going off trekking in Nepal on my own sounds fantastic, but the likelihood I'd actually do that is nil." He admires "adventurous types of people," Jack said, "but adventure doesn't have to mean jumping out of airplanes. It can just mean not doing the same things you've always done." Package tours for him and his wife sounded manageable, a comfortable way to gratify some of his wanderlust.

Jack thought he understood now why his initial forays into volunteer work, in a hospital and in a soup kitchen, had given him little satisfaction: "People moving through quickly, different volunteers around each time you go, not enough chance to make a real connection with anyone." No chance to be an educator (and a bit of a hero). He came up with a better idea, becoming a literacy volunteer ("that one-on-one effort over an extended period, seeing the progress, that appeals to me") — and he's just completed the application forms. Tutoring will actually probably prove to be an excellent fit for him; although working independently with each student, he'll feel secure as part of a structured program.

Jack is making his game plan.

ISABELLA, 45
communications director for a medical
equipment manufacturer

"I am an aunt," said Isabella with a laugh, and bet me that no one else I'd talked to had come up with that primary identity (which was true). With no children of her own, Isabella has lavished much time and attention on her eleven nieces and nephews, who range in age from two to eighteen. The importance of that role in her life somewhat took her by surprise: "I love being with those kids, but I never realized just how much or that being a good aunt is something I value so highly." Of her other roles — "good friend in need" and "loving sibling" were two of them — "corporate communications associate director does not in any way make the list," she said. "That's a title, and a fairly inane one at that."

Isabella checked off "nice people" as a big payoff from the job, then decided none of the other items on her list were especially meaningful to her. Taking not a great deal of intrinsic satisfaction from what she does for a living, Isabella finds that a great deal of what she likes about work these days has to do with externals — a place to exercise, its being near home so she can zip to and from in her car, a good cafeteria.

Much influenced by her father, the would-be English professor, Isabella achieved her earliest applause and status on the homefront by working hard in school, being "a little brain," attending a prestigious college. Although her career has involved literary kinds of effort — editing books, writing speeches and other corporate materials —

she doesn't think now that intellectual activities will be a main source of satisfaction for the future. "I like to read, like anybody," she said, "but nothing too heavy. I used to think scholarly pursuits were the highest good, but in fact I've never been a scholarly person. I'm a physical person."

Admiring her intellectual father and very bright, very "focused" older brother, she's really more like her "sensuous" mother: "What makes me happy? Being in the ocean. Knitting. Having a couple of little kids sitting on my lap and reading to them. Messing around with food, baking cookies and bread. I probably should have done something completely different with my life, like train to be a sous chef."

That bothers her still — the nagging notion that she headed off on a wrong track years ago and never booted herself off it. Getting out of college "without a clue of what comes next" was a major turning point for Isabella, at which the previously very clear, overachieving path she'd been on came to a sudden halt. She thinks now that some guidance during her later school years might have sent her along a more satisfying career route, instead of one she "basically backed into, out of fear I'd never get a job and out of a lack of any bright thought about what I could do or wanted to do."

Still, she's got a bit of a gambler's spirit. She lived in Paris for two years, jaunted around Europe on the cheap, had some adventures. "My little experiment in international living is something I'm proud of myself for doing," she said. "I've never been an excessively cautious person, but neither would I call myself a major risk taker. And that was a risk." So was getting divorced: "There was nothing terribly wrong with my marriage, and nothing terribly right, either. And I decided that wasn't good enough for a life with someone."

Although she's allowed herself to stay stuck in a kind of work that has never felt to her like a good fit, she is in fact very much in charge of herself in many ways. "If I think of some of these items on your list — proceeding independently, overcoming obstacles, feeling a sense of achievement," she said, "in terms of my work life I'd have to conclude I come up mostly with roadblocks. Looking at the other areas of my life in those terms, I feel pleased with myself." She manages her finances well, entertains her friends with enthusiasm, likes living alone, sews some of her own stylish clothes. "And I have no problem proceeding independently into a restaurant I want to try," she said, "and ordering dinner and wine for one."

Isabella has the right stuff to take another gamble or two in the future, once she comes up with some choices and goals that sing to her.

HOW ISABELLA REVIEWED
HER RETIREMENT DREAMS

Remembering her childhood fantasies about being a nun in a leper colony, Isabella, with a laugh, appreciated her heightened sense of melodrama as a youngster. She realized something else as well: "This nurturing or taking-care-of theme has been the consistent and significant aspect of my life, in the midst of the inconsistent and not so significant aspects. In adulthood it's mainly through my relatives, especially my nieces and nephews, who are my great joy."

Her best times, she said, always revolved around the crowded, noisy, funny messiness of life with her extended family and many friends: "What I imagined for the future seems to concern escape — faraway houses by the sea, spiritual retreats, sitting in a little atelier somewhere restoring fine art. Even one of my most-admired people was an editor I worked with who had plans to quit work and go cross-country with her husband on their motorcycles. Escape. It's all about the opposite of what I do and where I am. I haven't considered my ministering, nurturing needs. Cozy needs."

She thought that out a bit further, recognizing that the nieces and nephews will grow up, the next generation will surely be somewhat more removed. "Even if I remarry," Isabella said, "I doubt I'm going to have kids of my own. And I really do like being around little children!" Her generative need, she realized, was a powerful motivator for her life.

A lightbulb went on: "I have, probably, another fifteen or twenty working years ahead of me," Isabella said. "That's a lot of time coming up, especially to be doing something I don't especially enjoy. I don't have a pile of money at the moment, but I have enough; the condo and the car are paid for, I have investments. If I'm ever going to take a big chance, now is the time." Isabella began thinking about a career change, "something that never really occurred to me as a possibility before. But I was always a good student, I have no problem with the idea of going back to school. And I know if I start it, I'll finish it."

At age forty-five, Isabella is at a good place from which to consider switching to a more gratifying kind of work, and can afford a phasing-in period of reeducation. She did some exploratory checking into three possibilities: first, art restoration, the notion that had intrigued her "for about fifteen minutes [back] in college" and that was still on her mind, and concluded that the study was "too intense, not for me." She looked into the training program offered by a culinary institute, and decided against it: "I remember reading an interview with Marcella Hazan, my idol, in which she said that when she retired from writing cookbooks and giving workshops, she wanted to have the pleasure of preparing a fantastic meal just for her husband and watching his face as he took the first bites. That's the pleasure in it for me, feeding my nearest and dearest. I knew instantly all the fun would go out of cooking if I *had* to do it."

Her third possibility: early child development. That one appealed to her.

Deciding to begin a graduate program, Isabella was working out ways to adjust her work hours around a course or two when another lightbulb went on. She applied for a six-month sabbatical from her job, was granted it, and prepared to spend half a year back in school. "This may not lead to any major change, the career switch may never actually happen," she said. "I may never *work* in another field, but I can equip myself for the possibility. Maybe sometime set up an after-school program at the middle school in my town, teach the kids some art." Plus she's sure that getting away from the job for a while will send her back to it refreshed.

"I wasn't completely off the mark," she said about her retirement dreams. "I still want a lot of ocean time in the future! But something more, too."

MAX, 58
vice president with a food company

About his identity, Max said with a laugh, "Mainly, I'm still what I was forty-five years ago, a neurotic boy from Brooklyn trying to make people smile." Then, talking about his various roles, he wanted to hold on to "being a good husband, because I think I finally got that one right" and to "vice president, because that's a title that means I made something of myself, and it's gonna scare me to lose it." And Max surprised himself by listing son and brother. "This is interesting," he said, "because my father and one of my brothers are gone now, and being son and brother to those two people are the roles I'd really like to get rid of and are the roles that still seem to have me by the throat!" Family issues loom large and not always happily: "The fact that my father never thought a whole lot of me, all that sibling rivalry. I really need to put that to rest in my own head."

He's "never been much of a great thinker; I'd rather see a show or go out dancing than read a book." But some of his most satisfying accomplishments — studying for an MBA relatively late in life, "having a good head for numbers" — required intelligence and grit, and he takes pride in that.

Nor did Max feel any strong draw or compulsion toward physical activity. "Once a few years ago, I decided I was going to make the next twelve months the Year of the Body," he said. "I got very serious about eating right; I went jogging, lifted weights." He trimmed down and toned up; he's still pretty trim and toned and still eating right, but after the Year of the Body was over, he drifted away from his workouts: "That stuff is a bore. Dancing is the only physical activity that's fun for me."

Max tended to make intense but somewhat short-lived friendships. "The friends were always connected with the jobs, but when the jobs went, the friends sort of went, too. I'm not a great guy for keeping in touch with people." That's an area he thought he ought to improve, he said, "because I get a lot of warmth from getting to know some of the people at work, having lunch with some of them, just kind of hanging around shooting the bull when we've been working late." He was going to miss that.

Although he was "the pied piper" when his daughters were little, Max feels he hasn't really connected with them as young adults — "I love them, they love me, but we don't have a lot to say." He'd like them now to understand where he comes from and what has shaped him, and what in turn has shaped them, he said.

"Do I need applause and recognition?" said Max. "Always!" Making people laugh was how he distinguished himself as a youngster and started him along his fantasy path, another Sid Caesar or Jackie Gleason. Looking back over his career turning points, he realized applause and recognition, or his perceived lack thereof, directed some of his moves. "I've had a lot of difficulty with authority figures over the years," he said, "the professors in college, the bosses at work. On jobs, if I didn't get a promotion I was after or I didn't get a lot of pats on the back, I'd say, Screw this, and leave." But moving on wasn't a bad thing: "I've always been ready to take a new risk, pull up stakes, try something else."

Max felt he's been good at calling his own shots over the years, beginning with going to college despite any encouragement, and certainly in choosing a career in show business, a radical departure from anything his family considered appropriate. "My choices didn't always pan out," he said, "but they were mine." He's a self-starter, too: "I can get myself going, I don't need other people pushing me. Once I figure out what the goal is."

Looking ahead, he thought that was going to be his biggest roadblock. "On three occasions in the past I've set myself very fixed goals. First, to be some kind of real hotshot in TV. Second, to do live comedy. Third, to become a psychoanalyst. In hindsight now, I think none of those were realistic. They were over the top, or I just wasn't cut out for it, or my emotional life was getting in the way of reaching them. Whatever I do next, it's got to be in the realm of the possible."

Max needed to start giving more weight to what he *had* achieved, however, and perhaps ease up on himself about his "failures." Tracing out his career path, he said, brought that notion home to him: "If you asked me before, I'd probably have said I'm not a finisher, I didn't follow through on those goals I had. But, in fact, I can say I've been doing a damn good job in my business for a long time now, I'm a hard worker, I got somewhere."

HOW MAX REVIEWED HIS RETIREMENT DREAMS

Max thought one of the possibilities that had first occurred to him — dancing — was, in fact, an excellent choice, and he took action immediately. Starting twice-a-week dance classes at a local club, he was having a lot of fun: "We do West Coast swing, the lindy, the savoy, something called triple time. I see it as performing, which of course is what I just love to do." His wife isn't enthused about the activity herself, but Max has found a partner (with an equally uninterested spouse), and the two think at some point they might be good enough to enter competitions.

He might even be good enough to teach dance himself, Max decided and was excited by a newspaper article his wife clipped: "There's a guy, I think he was an ex-marine or something, who liked to dance, got serious about lessons, started teaching it, now hires himself out on cruise boats a couple of times a year as a dance instructor." His wife suggested that Max would probably have a grand time doing the same, and then they both got excited. "Dancing and cruising," he said, "what a combination. My wife loves going places, and for me, it kind of conjures up a couple of great years in the past."

Looking over his autobiography, thinking about the turning points and the times he felt most comfortable with himself, Max realized that the three years he spent in the Caribbean were among his happiest: "That period was always colored in my mind by the thought, Well, I had to do it because the old man was pressuring me, because otherwise my older brother was going to end up with the whole business, all that rivalry stuff. But, in fact, I mostly loved living in the islands, loved the free-form kind of days." He wondered if he and his wife should look into buying a little condo somewhere, spend a couple of months a year there.

Writing his memoirs he meant as kind of a joke when he originally suggested it, Max said, but now he began thinking, Why not? And what better way, perhaps, to sort out the family pressures and rivalries, and loosen the hold of his old son and brother roles finally? And maybe his daughters *would* want to read it when he was finished, and maybe that would bring them closer.

The thing that focused him briefly years back on the possibility of becoming an analyst, he said, was stumbling across a copy of *Man's Search for Himself* by Rollo May, "and that's what I've been doing for years and am still doing, searching for myself. But I can see this memoir idea now as more of a family history. Get into genealogy, do some research, talk about what it was like coming over to this country for my parents. Write about those characters I remember as a kid, my most unforgettable people, the crazy grandparents and aunts and uncles and other relatives."

He saw writing their history as in keeping with his continuing interest in psychology, "even the touchy-feely stuff, what makes people do what they do." It might even be a route to a kind of psychological liberation and becoming that "full-fledged adult" he wants to be, a way to make sense of and organize lingering feelings — regret, anger, guilt — that got in the way of his growing up: "Three-quarters of what I've been like all my life and still am comes from those people, the good and the bad of that family and that culture. Instead of running away from that, I can run to it."

Preliminary information-gathering — through the International Genealogical Index, the U.S. Immigration and Naturalization Service, and other sources — produced such a wealth of rich material that Max said he was "jazzed! Amazing stuff to be uncovered! And, as I've discovered about myself, I have a good head for detail, putting the pieces together." Planning trips to the National Archives and Ellis Island and working up descendancy charts on his new computer software, Max delighted in the unfolding story that could occupy him for years to come.

It would have a lot of drama, he thought, and a lot of comedy, too.

SHEILA, 55
senior partner in a law firm

Thinking about our identity statement, Sheila said: "I am a lawyer, I guess." She found her most persuasive identification from a job she pursues in a field she doesn't love ("I am not enamored of the law"), perhaps largely because other areas of her life were not terribly vital or emotionally sustaining at the moment.

But from that job she is ambivalent about, she draws her main intellectual stimulation, a key component to her feeling of well-being and one of her most important positive payoffs from work. Sheila was always an outstanding student, first in her class; even today, "learning something new" and "improving my brain" is the primary means of preventing the boredom that periodically overcomes her. Whatever she does in the future, clearly it will have to enable her to employ her keen intelligence — and she knows that's got to be more than "just reading books."

Besides helping people, work felt the best when she was moving on, "not stagnating"; lately, however, she's bothered by the sense of "coasting." There are too many days, she said, "that either I'm unhappy being at work or I'm just flat." Sheila clearly isn't the best candidate to keep the job going into her senior years, although as a lawyer it's her call; indeed, she thinks now that it's a mistake to stay in one field all one's life — "it's too long." And yet, she said, "I'll keep working if I absolutely can't come up with anything else, because I would be very afraid not to have something to get me out of bed in the morning."

A while back she started thinking of "the necessity to do some exercise in my life, and eat more healthily than I used to," and some light working out is an activity she and her husband share. But physical activity has never been a particular pleasure for Sheila and is unlikely to be so in the future — unless she can stop going at it in her conscientious, determined way for the sake of "good health."

From being an extremely religious kid, Sheila described herself now as "extremely irreligious. Religion plays almost no role in my life." But she loved it once, named it one of her reigning childhood passions, regrets that it slipped away over the years, and misses the rituals. In considering what part, if any, spiritual attentions should play in her future, she first thought that would be a passion impossible to recapture: "I feel that the central core is missing, which is that belief in God. I'm too rational now, and rituals without belief would probably be meaningless."

Sheila is no lone wolf. She enjoys interaction with people — indeed, she craves them — and one of her "I'm best at" aspects of her career has been "relating to people." Still, she hasn't found much satisfaction in serving on community boards and such; being one of a group in those endeavors isn't to her liking. Volunteering, she said, "is really not me."

She loved her intense mothering years, but there's not much call on those emotions and energies these days. She feels no strong pull, she said, to "pass on the baton" to any younger generation, although she thought having grandchildren someday would be nice, a day she's not sure will arrive.

Considering our 1 to 10 activity level scale, from couch potato to whirling dirvish, Sheila rated herself a 5. "I do like downtime," she said, "where I can sit and read and not be pressured. But I also get anxious with too much of that, and I need to go out and socialize with my friends." Her overall energy level is low. Without the job to get her out the door in the morning, she said, "I tend to inertia." Without the job in the future, she worried, "I'd vegetate."

Her work at times has involved high elements of risk — "going into court, trying cases, many murder cases and capital crimes, having someone's future dependent on the job I was doing, knowing how I'd feel if I was unsuccessful." But the job changes along her "Careers" map didn't feel risky to her, only opportunities to learn something new and keep mentally alert. Now in midlife she considers herself "not especially courageous at all."

Making choices hasn't been a problem for Sheila — she'll take action, although throughout her working career she's tended to reach for opportunities only as they presented themselves. On her own, she's been less than successful at initiating action, waiting until restlessness or ennui propel her to see friends, slipping into that inertia that bedevils her. She's good at changing course, but again, it's when she sees boredom setting in that she moves on — always, also, within the limits of the law that she's "not enamored of," feeling perhaps stymied, just as her father did.

With her strongly idealistic and altruistic nature and with the powerful lessons she learned in her parents' home, she set for herself the highest of goals way back in high school: "I was going to change the world." She was also, she said, "going to make one of these magnificent marriages, to someone also very important. An ambassador, perhaps, and we'd be working together on that level." Although she can acknowledge that she's done solid and useful work over the years, Sheila has a deeply felt sense of not having achieved what she could have; she calls herself not "a huge success," because if you're successful, you're happy, and she's often not.

When she finds the right vehicles for expression — "something that truly engrosses me," she said — Sheila has real strengths to bring to the table. She's a hard worker, her follow-through is excellent. Her concerns now that she's "not much of a self-starter" may very well fade once she gets going.

How Sheila Reviewed Her Retirement Dreams

At first, going back to her page one was a dispiriting exercise. "I have no dream," she said. "I can't think of where to look. Don't want to take courses. Don't like community activism. This is a pretty pathetic picture! I'm envious of people who have these wonderful hobbies, things they love to do."

But in thinking over her autobiography so far, Sheila was struck by how often she used that word *passion,* and what it meant to her: "I did use to have passions when I was younger, powerful ones." Social activism was important to her, but so was her involvement in her temple, Hebrew speaking camp — "I very much identified myself as a Zionist, I had a great belief in God, a great spirituality." And so were the plays she wrote; she used to *love* writing, she said, used to love reading fiction and poetry. "Getting back in touch with the creative, spiritual, not-so-rational elements of my nature," she said, "is probably just what I most need." Even lately, the passions flare up — she can be "revolted" by reading accounts of the inequities that exist in the world.

And then, considering our list of activators, she pointed to what she believed was her major roadblock: "Setting reasonable goals. I haven't mentally figured out what that might mean in these areas that once absorbed me." Sheila may have hit the nail on the head. In discovering ways to reclaim old passions, she first needed to put effort into adjusting her sights regarding goal setting, finding satisfaction in less lofty, all-or-nothing accomplishments.

Certainly those accomplishments had to in some manner involve "doing good," a key component in her liberal nature and her view of the well-lived life. Sheila has to a great extent always equated a sense of achievement with being socially useful. But for a woman who once wanted to "change the world," more modest improvements tend to be unsatisfying — perhaps the reason her work life has often left her feeling unhappy and "flat."

In wrestling with these ideas, Sheila discovered a wonderfully useful role model in her much admired mother. She recalled that her mother — who always wanted to be a creative writer, took courses, never got published, and worked in a series of unrelated jobs — found a great contentment later in life: "In her last years she wasn't terribly well, and there were a number of things she couldn't do anymore. But what gave her enormous pleasure was that she started to write a weekly column for the local paper about community affairs — she was like the little old lady activist, sounding out on the need for additional traffic lights, evening hours at the library. She felt she was contributing something important. And she was."

Sheila's heroes, aside from her mom, always tended to be larger than life; if she could stop measuring herself against the Eleanor Roosevelts (and realize her husband was never going to be a Franklin), she could find in her adored mother a model much more cut down to size. Her mother brought her own goals down a notch, and Sheila thought she could do something similar: "For one thing, maybe simply participating in the rituals of my religion might be enough for now. I might get pleasure and comfort out of that, even if the central core, the belief, is not so strong as it once was and maybe will never come back."

She wondered, too, if contributing her knowledge and experience and her excellent problem-solving skills to pro bono work for, perhaps, an international relief organization would be a good course of action for the future: "I'm not one for standing around like a smiling idiot dispensing popcorn at the holiday fair, but I can probably find something less trivial." She lets herself get discouraged, she said, even "despair" at all that needs to be done, but she planned to make an effort to fight back those feelings: "I remember reading something Margaret Mead said, when she was asked if a small number of people or a small movement can make a difference. And she said, 'It's the only thing that ever has.' I think that's the right mind-set."

And maybe, she thought, it would be good to drag up from the basement that carton of plays and stories she had so enjoyed writing long ago, read through them, and consider how she might rekindle that particular spark. The lawyer who was also an artist, the lawyer who was also restoring an old house, another who wrote plays — they were people she most admired and envied, and she wished she hadn't let her own creative nature wither on the vine.

Now, although she didn't want to move too far afield, traveling any distance or sitting through evening classes, Sheila made a few phone calls and found a creative-writing instructor at a nearby college who was more than willing to be hired for an occasional at-home tutorial. He also suggested that at some point she might want to join a writing workshop he knew about, a small group of women who got together every so often and read out loud their works in progress.

We came up with another thought: this is a woman with a restless soul in a restless body. She hates being penned up, feeling confined (among the "what I most dislike" aspects of her work), and she gets angry with herself when she feels she's been "just sitting around," but when she's not working, she mostly does sit around reading. She'd probably experience a keen sense of pleasure from the kinds of physical pursuits she's never indulged, even just some long, unplanned walks. All her life she has been patted on the back for everything she "accomplished" in a day. She would do well now to assign value to casual leisure, and tell herself it's not being slothful.

Sheila felt all this was doable, if she kept her eye on small forward steps rather than on overwhelming goals and on the need always to feel things "on the gut level." It was starting to sound exciting to her.

BARRY, 66
investor, consultant, arts critic, retired manufacturer

"I am a liberator, liberating the creative energy and reorienting the brains of other business people!" said Barry with a laugh, in response to our identity question. Barry takes great pride in doing many and difficult things exceptionally well — not only very well but more successfully than anyone else. To "measure up against others, and be better" was a top payoff from the job. Much of his working life, and indeed, his great pleasure, has involved telling people what to do, having them do it, and gaining the satisfaction of seeing his solutions work. "When they implement my recommendations and things happen," he said, "that turns me on." He needs prestige, status, and if not power, recognition.

Barry is bright, creative, with many interests. Knowing that intellectual pursuits keep him going, he made sure he'd have his fingers in several pies once he left corporate life, to provide the "mental concentration" he craves. Although officially retired, he's working as many hours as ever, which is how he wants it — as a dance and music critic (with his own byline!), money manager, consultant — "strategic management development, strategic planning, implementing, finding the niche for a business." Barry has taken his considerable smarts and talents and found these several postwork paths in which to continue to prove his worth.

Some of his time is occupied with tennis, which he plays three or four afternoons a week, mainly to stay healthy. But that's an avenue, too, in which he can give vent to his highly competitive nature, "be better" than the next guy, play the game like his hero Jackie Robinson, "always looking for that little competitive edge." As with his tennis partners, his relationships are mainly business-related (and often competitive); interpersonal relationships are not a vital part of his life. He's aware that his family attachments haven't always been especially satisfactory and that he never struck an especially rewarding balance between work and family. Consequently, he's taking the grandfather role more seriously these days. But most of his generative focus has been directed elsewhere — especially, "liberating creative energy" in other business types.

We'd think of Barry as on the whirling-dervish end of the activity-needs scale, although he claims he's comfortable at both ends. He doesn't have a spot on the 1 to 10 scale, he said, but "multiple spots. I love the extremes. I love getting involved in a situation that requires a level of effort that no one human being I know could ever match! And I love absolutely just stopping and going to the other extreme. I have no problem with that, either." Barry doesn't stop for long, however. His skydiving nature gets him going again.

This is a man who has been at risk since childhood, "a scared kid with no ambitions," putting all his energies into "day-to-day, emotional survival" in a confined household with a difficult parent, and looking back, he saw all his major moves as fraught with risk: "Starting in high school, in among these incredibly gifted kids, not knowing if I could measure up. Big risk!" Over his career, all the turning points were defined by a high element of chance: "Not taking a sure job in the chemical area and starting up a business I didn't know a damn thing about. Not even knowing how to start a business. Buying out the business that had been my parent company, knowing how many things were wrong with it. Betting the company three separate times, when if I was wrong, I'd be wiped out."

Barry has many strong suits going for him. Clearly, he thrives on making choices; indeed, as long as a path is one of his own choosing, he likes it and is a wholehearted self-starter, setting his own time frames, answering to no one, working through the night if he wants to. He's not above asking for information when he needs it, like when he explored the meaning of retirement with a psychologist, but ever since childhood, he hasn't liked being told what to do or having demands put on him; that gives him "a fit."

He sets his goals very high; in fact, they can't be high enough to suit him, but not reaching some energizes rather than deflates him. Golf, he said (a game he hasn't taken up because he needs more calorie burning, which he accomplishes on the tennis court), "would be ideal for me, because it's an unattainable idea. You keep pushing toward something better, which meets my needs perfectly. I'd never be satisfied until I got to a zero handicap, which I'd never get to."

When Barry contemplated our question about valuing pleasure and allowing himself to seek it, he said he's having as much fun now as he's ever had — working. He can knock off and enjoy some of that downtime. "And I can walk away anytime I want. I say to myself about once a year, when I get really aggravated, I don't have to do any of this." But it's clear that for him work *is* fun. He read an interview with Tom Brokaw, he said, about his book *The Greatest Generation:* "Brokaw was talking about his father, and he said, 'Work defined him in every way. It was how he made his living and it was his favorite leisure-time activity.' The same holds true for me."

In his life, he has been most comfortable with himself right now: "I don't fight the demons. I accept my limitations. I'm doing almost only the things I like."

How Barry Reviewed His Retirement Dreams

"Perfectly satisfied," he declared. "I think I doped it out pretty well. What I thought I would need to do to keep myself happily occupied turned out to be exactly right." He feels especially pleased that he was able to incorporate the arts, one of his earliest interests and loves, into his after-the-job life in a dynamic and involving way: "If I was doing all money managing and consulting, I wouldn't be satisfied. All left-brain stuff. Art is right brain."

Barry *should* feel satisfied. And all that he's up to now

should keep working well for him . . . until something changes. What then? I asked, and Barry immediately got the idea. "What you're really outlining here," he said, "is a model for preparing for transitions you know are coming, a lifelong process of re-creating yourself as circumstances change. So, ten, twenty years from now, if I'm still here, knock wood, what circumstances will have changed?"

He hoped to be still essentially robust and healthy but imagined his energy level would not be what it is today; some physical infirmities might be creeping in; his eyesight, never very good, would be worse. "I think it'd be a good idea to go through some of the same steps of preparation," Barry said, "getting information, evaluating what's important to me, what my resources are going to be, what different assumptions are going to come into play that I ought to be ready for. Learning lessons from the negatives, asking, Is this the natural state of affairs, or can it be changed?"

He's well aware that he thrives on intense involvement in very specific activities that he loves. He can do some thinking now, he said, about what he'd most comfortably let go of, or how to keep active in a more toned-down way. That's always been his best asset, Barry thought: "Look at what's working for me, shuck off the rest, keep moving the jigsaw pieces around to come up with the right picture."

THERESA, 58
retired management supervisor in an oil company

"I am a good daughter, a good wife, a good friend," Theresa said. And she is, from early childhood days cleaning and cooking and being obedient, to the kind and thoughtful adult she became. She's a listener, a caretaker, a woman who believes that above all it's important to be fair to others.

She's intelligent but considers herself in the shadow of her much admired older sister, "the smart one." Still, Theresa puts a high value on her own sense of curiosity and eagerness to learn — she'd "always ask how something worked and why it worked," and she's proud of that instinct. A major turning point on her career path came with the introduction of computers, when she sought to find out what they could do. When the computer experts told her they could program anything she could think up, Theresa saw the possibilities and took advantage of them. Using her mind creatively on the job made her feel great; now, after the job, she hasn't found ways to replace that intellectual involvement.

Nor has she been able to find satisfaction from putting to use her strong skills as a manager, of things and people. "I manage my husband's and my finances, pay the bills, and so on," she said. "It doesn't take much time or effort." Theresa likes to "be in charge"; in her last position at work, she felt the most comfortable with herself that she had ever been, because she supervised people, she had power, and she used it well. These days there's not much that she can be in charge of.

The job, indeed, gave her such a lot. Within a large corporate facility where she felt protected and comfortable, she found her major source of friendship and support; the place was "like a family," people helping one another out, joking, talking. The job was her learning field, really; it was there she found out about people, what made them tick. She felt liked by others, and being liked and appreciated is important to her. It was there, too, that she stretched her wings, moving up through an apprenticeship system to an extent she never anticipated at the start, feeling at the end she might even have made vice president, had she come in at a different time.

She's only lately realized how much she misses the camaraderie of the office, too. Theresa married late, having lived with her mother well into her adulthood, she has no children, and although her marriage is a happy one, Theresa's a talker — "I'll talk to anybody and they talk to me, I even talk to the TV screen" — and her husband isn't. A deeply religious woman, she continues to draw sustenance from her daily churchgoing but hasn't found ways to expand that involvement.

She's a woman who really wants to be very, very active — tempted to grab her briefcase and follow all those people she watched heading off to work — but whose risk level is very, very low.

Theresa has never made strong choices in her life, such as defying her mother and pursuing her wish to study nursing, never initiated much action on her own. Personal discipline and the dictates of others defined her path. But when opportunities were presented to her, as they were on the job, she grabbed them and ran.

Not an aggressive person, restricted by an interrupted education and an opinionated parent, she nevertheless managed to make lemonade out of lemons. Through her competence and attitude, she achieved what she considers a large measure of success. And she could be assertive and initiate action on behalf of others — taking charge of the family counseling program in the nursing home her mother was confined to and improving the quality of care, sticking up for employees she supervised when she felt they were inadequately treated. She calls herself nonconfrontational, one who always shied away from an argument, but when she had to speak out on the job — "because it was about being fair" — she could do it.

Theresa's delight in the freedom of this time in her life — "You know, I just want to do what I want! Because I never could do that!" — is real and powerful, and a voice she is right to heed. She wants to call her own shots, she's saying, finally. But it's a mixed blessing. Although she relished free time, an indulgence she'd never enjoyed before, all that time without the powerful payoffs she had relied on for so long turned out to be disappointing. She's keenly aware of a lack of purposeful action in her days.

How Theresa Reviewed
Her Retirement Dreams

Theresa didn't have to mull over her retirement dreams very long; she had been living them for a year, and she knew they weren't adding up to a tremendously satisfying picture.

Gardening, cooking, shopping, cleaning — that kept her busy but was a long way from meeting her deepest motivators.

However, she still felt strongly about that notion of holding on to the freedom she'd never before enjoyed. "After going through this exercise with you," she said, "I thought, I never wanted to quit working, I *had* to, so why don't I think about getting another job? But not the way I did it before. Not full-time and not the whole focus, not the thing that I shape my week and my whole life around." She wanted to feel reckless and indulgent sometimes, which for Theresa meant hitting the sales on a Monday or poking around for an afternoon getting together the ingredients for a new recipe she wanted to try — or just, she said, "enjoying my home, looking around at six-thirty or seven in the evening, I've taken my shower, my house is all cleaned, the dishes are done, and I think, Wow, the rest of the night is mine. I really get a lot of pleasure out of that."

Thinking "why not another job?" was enormously liberating for her. First, she hadn't recognized before just how much she relied on work, not only for income and self-image but for small pleasures — joking, talking, connecting with people. And second, "the job" had always been defined by "the company," the place she had worked since her high school days and the place that essentially, then, decreed her working days were over. Now, she came up with another way to look at work.

Theresa took action; she called a man who had also "been retired" from the company and whom she knew had taken a new management job at a homeowner's insurance company. She said, "Frank, I want to work. Any ideas?" and was hired the next week as a part-time customer service rep — ironically, the one job she had been passed over for in her work life.

She found herself thinking a lot, too, about the old dream of becoming a nurse; she had forgotten how powerfully it had pulled her in her teens. She began volunteering in a hospice ("emptying bed pans, just like my mother said") and there she found a satisfying outlet for important motivators — being with people, helping family members, listening, talking, doing something good for people who are badly off. "I get more than I give there," she said. "I get very positive personal relationships with people."

But still the need for her own freedom was a siren call. After spending long hours with several hospice clients, Theresa decided to limit her involvement to twice a week for a couple of hours each: "I want time for myself now. For once in my life I'm going to take it."

Eventually, Theresa might get real satisfaction by taking the level of her involvement in her churchgoing and hospice activity up a notch, leading some groups of like-minded people in one worthwhile cause or another. She might train new hospice volunteers to work with clients, or head up a women's fund-raising organization at church. She feels good when she can "be in charge" and use her strengths as a manager.

Running the show in one of these ways, Theresa might get back a little of that sense of power she used to enjoy and now misses — and she might find it a lot easier to "accept life better" and feel successful again.

DAVE, 64
retired talent agent

He's "a family man, first and foremost," Dave said, and "a theater person to the depths of my soul." Being a theater person — producing, directing, or managing plays or films — was all he ever wanted, "the absolute preoccupation of my heart," even as a child. But feeling pressured by his parents — "their message was always 'You can't figure things out on your own, Dave; you can't be out on the streets of the world'" — and not ever quite having the confidence to follow the dream, Dave felt frustrated and dissatisfied with his career path: "Almost all of what I've done as a job has involved being on the sidelines of where I wanted to be. Being in a service role to creative people who were having creative lives, like I should have had."

And yet he looks back at his working days and can feel good about much that he sees. Although he still beats himself up for "not working hard enough all along, not having my heart in it, should have made a lot more money," Dave also gives himself some pats on the back: "I succeeded at what I was doing; I could be the person totally in charge. I'm very proud of the skills I developed, negotiating skills especially. I was enormously competent — competent for clients, competent for friends in the business, always there to help. I can truthfully say there were things I was exceptional at, in recognizable ways." The work, he said, was just never what he wanted.

Retirement, he thought, and the chance to live that "civilized, urbane, relaxed life," *would* be just what he wanted. So far, it hadn't been turning out the way he planned, though not for lack of ideas. This is a man whose motivators are extensive and strongly felt — to be mentally and physically engaged, to ride his bike and go to the gym and play tennis, to keep his many friendships vital and enjoyable, to be with his family, to pursue his creative hobbies, to give attention to his "neglected spiritual life." Indeed, his cup runneth over with all the matters that call to him. How to get a grip on them, that's his challenge. "For somebody who has so many books to read, so much music to learn, so much time I want to spend being a fine husband, committed for the rest of our lives, being a model grandparent to my grandchildren, for somebody who has places to go, so much good to do in the world . . . I need focus," he said. "I need to clear my head."

Considering our list of activators, a little clarity dawned. Dave immediately identified what he considered major roadblocks in his path: "First, I have never been good at making choices, making my own decisions, except on the job, because there I didn't have the luxury of not making them. Second, setting goals is a toughie. My big goals haven't panned out — getting a life in the theater, making enough money so I could quit working at age fifty and take my wife and myself off to see the world. So apparently I am not a good setter of goals.

"And most important, I am not much of a self-starter and I am not happy going it alone. Without feedback, I flounder."

Dave had a pretty good handle on what was getting in his way. "To start," he said, "I really have to get over the old resentment about my parents steamrolling me about *real* jobs and the white picket fence, and get over not making enough money. It's all water under the bridge." He can do that, he thought: "I earned as much money as I deserved to for how hard I was willing to work, which is kind of uncomfortable to say. But it's all right. I provided for my family, nobody starved and nobody's going to starve in the future, and I was always enormously satisfied with the balance in my life — great friends, my hobbies, travel, the arts."

That's the attitude he needs to keep. Dave has a tendency to look at the negative — "things didn't turn out the way I thought they would turn out" — and then mention the positive as an afterthought. He'd give himself a break by bringing the positive to the fore, remembering that the focus of his life was always outside the job, which is where he wanted it.

But feedback is the bigger roadblock. Dave needs people around, not so much to give him applause and recognition but to anchor him in the here and now. All those phone calls — "Dave, I need you to do this . . . thanks for taking care of this . . . get back to me as soon as you can" — kept him fixed on the task at hand. In considering his career path, he remembered vividly the one point that gave him the most grief, the three years he worked independently, developing scripts: "The free-form nature of that, the individual effort, the absence of any structurally responsible feedback, your day being your own invention — it drove me crazy. I was ineffectual." The parallels are clear, he said, to what's going on now.

He calls himself a poor self-starter, but what he is really missing in these after-the-job days is that structure, the imposed schedule and routine around which he could "fit in" his enthusiasms. When he had to be showered, shaved, suited up and someplace by ten, Dave relished the earlier two hours at the piano and out on his bike.

Intense, serious, and introspective, he's been flailing lately. Once he finds some of those anchors, however, Dave's strong suits should serve him well. He's a creative guy who really does enjoy life, he's changed direction several times over his working career and can do so again if need be, and he's a finisher.

How Dave Reviewed His Retirement Dreams

Dave took another look at what he called his before and after picture. At first, for about six months, there was "liberation!" Then depression. "I certainly did have a vision," he said. "It never occurred to me beforehand that I'd be bored and unhappy." It came as a shock, then, that even things he used to love, like writing music and playing the piano, lost some of their charm. Based on his experience, he would offer this advice, he said, to anyone looking toward retirement: "You need to be prepared for psychological aspects that you don't expect. You need to deal with them, and not be embarrassed, ashamed, or frightened."

But he had already figured out for himself that the lack of any imposed structure made it hard to get himself organized, pin himself down. "So I'm imposing one on myself," he said. "I figure I need a minimum of three absolutely fixed activities each week, where I have to *get myself somewhere* and I have to be fully committed." He signed himself up for a private piano lesson, a group class in beginning music theory, and a course in music composition at a school of adult continuing education. "Paying money for these things will ensure that I get myself there," he said, "and maybe they'll help me get into a regular routine. Plus it's stuff I enjoy."

Dave had tried some things that were simply not rewarding; he gets easily disgusted by the politics of some group activities, even in his favored field of the arts. "That's one thing I know I don't want more of," he said, "joining these organizations, volunteering that time, as I did for a while at the art museum and a couple of other places. Sitting in meetings, listening to people jockeying for position."

But curiously, although a life in the theater is what he's always wanted, Dave never joined amateur groups in his community. Even as a young person, he "worshiped" various actors, playwrights, and theater directors, and he sees every play and film that opens. "I'm still sort of stuck back on the big goal that I missed," he said, "being a professional in that world."

Considering how he might come up with a related but more modest goal, he hit on a bold and very specific idea — organizing and producing a children's theater group in the religious school his grandchildren attend. He looked up an old friend, previously the drama director in a children's summer day camp, and together they began outlining some play ideas: "We've got a little skit called *The Birdies Ball,* great for five- and six-year-olds. And we're working up adaptations of *The Wizard of Oz* and *Pajama Game,* good for the nine and ten crowd."

Dave was giving less attention to "the who is the real Dave? issue," he said, "which is all to the good."

MAY, 84
psychologist in private practice

"Motherhood, wifehood, widowhood, a little grandparenthood, a career of selfhood — that one a very big hunk" is the way May identified her roles. She represents a cadre of women who, having taken family-raising detours, established themselves firmly in the workforce later in life; she began a full-time practice only when she was in her late fifties. Since the career lives of most people span forty years, May thought — "if my good genes continue to serve me well" — she might have another fruitful ten years on the job.

This is not a woman who happened into a career; the choice was clear as a bell from childhood on, even "before it had a name I could put to it." She fought to have it — battling through an educational system that wasn't especially encouraging to women, keeping her experience fresh and her contacts alive through part-time appointments while her children were young. She still *loves* what she does; she embraces her career with great pride. It satisfies her needs to "be nosy and learn about people, to listen." And she is, fortunately, in a field in which her wisdom is an asset and her age no impediment.

May is "toward the whirling-dervish end on the activity scale; I make myself about a seven. I can't sit around. Only recently, I've started to become more tired, which I resent, so I take some naps. Don't see patients in the evening."

She has quite obviously been anything but averse to taking risks and setting goals, starting back in her youth: "From being decreed to be a good little girl, then the fact that I defied my mother, who objected actively and no holds barred to my career. That was very difficult, and painful. But I did it." Her goals are modest now: "Keep working, keep close to the family, keep my health and my marbles."

How May Reviewed Her Retirement Dreams

She had no plans to retire, May had said at the beginning of her autobiographical exploration, and she said the same thing at the conclusion of it.

Looking again at her initial plans for the future, May thought it might be enjoyable to allot a little more time to some of her interests — photography, museum going, taking that trip to China. The idea of sitting in the house on the hill was no more appealing than before. She is putting in fewer hours some weeks, and takes more vacations these days to be with her family, but she'll quit, she said, "when people stop calling me for appointments." Retirement was a decision she wasn't going to make; it would be made for her when the phone stopped ringing. And it hasn't yet: "They still come. And each new patient is still a new fascination."

The autobiographical journey reminded her of old mentors along the way, the professors and supervisors who offered encouragement, advice, inspiration, and "ego ideals." She hadn't thought about those connections for a long time, May said, and she wondered now if she might assume that role herself: "I believe I continue to learn much from my patients, and maybe it's a good point to pass along some of that. I'll see if I can be in an advisory position to a graduate student or two at my old university."

She had spent time reflecting on this question, she said: "Is continuing to work something of a cop-out? Are the people who keep working people who can't figure out what to do with the rest of their lives?" May decided the decision, for her, was no cop-out; she still had a lot to offer, she said, and felt productive and happy.

One more thought had come to mind: "I wouldn't mind finding a boyfriend, although I know that's improbable. I actually did have one for a while a couple of years ago, but he started to lose his marbles."

My Retirement Dreams, Revisited

Back now to where *you* began, page one of your notebook — "What I will be doing when I am no longer spending most of my time at the work I am doing now."

Does what you envisioned at the start truly fit what you have learned about yourself in the course of our auto-biographical exploration?

About your dreams, can you say you were right on target? You knew yourself well, and the plans you had in mind will work?

On the other hand, does it seem now that those plans will not quite fill the bill? But some new ones have been revealed? Or you have seen ways to come up with a mix of activities that will better meet your various needs? In any case, you have accepted that life after the job calls for your robust attention, and you're ready to apply it. In the following chapter, we consider some ways to get started.

CHAPTER 8

GETTING STARTED, AGAIN

P erhaps after all this you have come face-to-face with what psychologist James Hillman in his book *The Soul's Code* calls your "acorn," your life's exceptional component or most deeply driving motivation.

Or if nothing on quite that grand a scale has been revealed, you have brought to the surface some talents, convictions, or deeply felt personal needs that the "official" work you have done for years did not encompass or satisfy. Perhaps you thought about a small interest you once enjoyed and see some ways you might return to it now, or you want to fill in a few missing pieces.

Such was the case for many of the individuals who explored their journeys with me. Here is what some of them had to say:

A nursing supervisor: "Jorge Luis Borges wrote a poem

when he was eighty-five, supposedly his last. In one line he calls himself 'one of those who never went to any place without a thermometer, a boiling water bag, an umbrella and a parachute.' In a nutshell, that has been me! Now I think it will be a terrible thing if I hit my old age without ever having done something bold, difficult, or dangerous. I need to be a little rash."

A professor of economics: "What I want to do is take all this textbook theory I have, and start a tiny business that I know absolutely nothing about, apply my theory to that. See if I could make it successful, and have some fun at it."

An office manager: "What I've gleaned from this auto-biography is that I'm an intensely competitive person and have never really had a satisfying channel for that. Certainly my job hasn't given it to me. I've always been pretty athletic, but I was never encouraged as a kid. Recently it came together when I watched my daughter on her college crew team, and I said, 'I want to do that!' I want to get out there with some other old ladies like me and row and win some races."

An insurance salesman: "What gets my juices flowing, as you put it, is what gets me mad, and that has always been in some form or other the reluctance of people to work for a common good. Here in Florida we voted yes on an amendment to clean up the Everglades, and no to a one-penny-a-pound tax on sugar to pay for it, supposedly because it was going to cost jobs, which it wasn't. What's wrong with people? My parents used to call me the Senator. So I'm thinking, If it's true that all politics is local, I can certainly find some way to bring out the political animal in me. Stop just sitting back and crabbing about how everything's going to hell in a handbasket."

An engineer: "I'm a specialist at heart who's lived a generalist's life. A scientist who ended up working mostly in administration and marketing. The people who have always fascinated me are the ones who developed rabid pre-occupations with a particular study or activity. It's going beyond interest or even passion, into obsession. What appeals to me is the depth, immersing yourself in a singular pursuit. I realize that's what I was heading for back in school. My various interests give me pleasure. But I want to find a way to get that depth."

A music teacher: "There is a human need for music. People have always wanted it in their lives. My family is from Scotland, and the Scots, of course, have their bag-pipes! I think exploring the culture of music and instruments could be an exciting way to learn more about your roots, about my roots."

A stockbroker: "What I have done as work has absolutely no redeeming social value. That is a lack in my growth as a human being, and I need to think now about involving myself in social causes."

These men and women knew what they were after. They had also acquired pretty clear pictures of the personal strengths or shortcomings that would help or might hinder them as they reached for new possibilities. Introspection and reviewing some personal history had taken them far. But each had, as yet, still hazy notions of how to get going.

To consider how you might get going, and what you may experience along the way, we'll imagine three stages to come. First (assuming a fixed retirement in the future, the day after which you are no longer going to the job), the honeymoon.

Once the honeymoon begins to pall, the testing-new-waters stage begins. Or if you have already for some time been thinking about motivators and activators and have been getting your feet wet, now you set those plans in motion in earnest.

Then, somewhere down the line, it may be necessary to get a second wind and readjust sights in order to keep on moving toward where you've headed.

Honeymooning

When we talked, Bill T. was a mere three weeks into retirement, after a highly successful thirty-year career with two companies, which included stints in advertising, marketing, development, sales, and finance. Leaving the job at this particular juncture wasn't his plan, but, he said, "they made me one of those offers you can't refuse." An insightful man, he knew he hadn't mentally prepared for this new and abruptly entered stage of life; however, he had a sense of how the following months might play out and instinctively anticipated those three stages.

Here's what he was up to:

"Right now I'm on vacation. It's the greatest! The best thing about retirement is I have no homework on the weekends. First time since I was in fourth grade, no homework on Saturdays. It's an incredible sense of being.

"I decided before I left my job that I would take a six-month sabbatical. Instead of rushing into some brand-new things, let myself have that time just to step back, think it all over. Because my goal is not to focus on what I want to do in the next two or three years but to figure out a really intelligent twenty-year plan for myself, since I think if all goes well, I've got at least another twenty productive years.

"But this vacation is not a problem! I don't have to be going, going, going all the time. I've been really good at occasionally doing nothing, being docile, watching rather than participating. And I am spending a fair amount of time at the moment doing nothing, lying on my back and staring up at the sky, thinking."

Bill had a great attitude. There's nothing wrong with taking time to relax, luxuriate, and enjoy the vacation and the absence of homework. Vacations, after all, are gratifying and refreshing. Honeymoons are delightful.

This may be for you a stretch of doing what feels like nothing much of anything at all. A former copyeditor spent a lot of time at her local video store during the first three months after leaving her job: "I had a thoroughly indulgent, indeed slothful daily routine. I went to the Greek coffee shop across the street every morning, had breakfast and read the papers and let the waiter keep refilling my cup. I watched a soap opera in the afternoon, took my two-mile walk, ended up back at the video store, and rented one movie. There were actually about ninety movies I wanted to see, and I did."

It may be a time during which you wish to devote yourself to the sublimely mundane. Looking toward the point she will leave the job at which she works ten-to-twelve-hour days, six days a week, an insurance industry analyst plans to clean house. As she described it, however, the effort signifies more than mere tidying up. "When I leave my career behind," she said, "I intend to reinvent myself. I am not yet sure exactly what this new incarnation will look like, but I am absolutely certain it must begin by ridding myself of the accumulation of past lives."

She expects to devote a good half a year to sorting through, throwing out, selling, storing, or giving away "stuff. Thirty years of my daily appointment calendars. My late parents' leatherette-bound sets of the collected works of classic writers, which my mother bought in a romantic spirit when they were first married and which they never read. My grandmother's good linen, which I have never used and never will. A trunkful of cloth from the time I used to sew. Old Playbills. My daughter's school uniforms from fifteen years ago. The empty tropical fish tanks.

"I fully anticipate that I am now ready to let go of most of these items that were once emotionally significant and sentimental. I will look at them, remember what they meant, smile, and let them go."

The honeymoon may be a time for a few splurges. A retired lab technician spent forty-five years working a job, raising three children, caring for aging parents, and finishing a college degree at age fifty-five. "Financial strains over the years never allowed some dreams to take precedence over the necessities of life," she said. "Once the kids were independent, the house was paid for, we had a little money to spare, I permitted myself some presents." She felt no guilty qualms over the tour of three-star restaurants in France, Spain, and Italy or over her newly installed hot tub, she said, "because I never played before. I never had fun and games. I never did what pleased me first."

Or your honeymoon stage may be a time, as it was for Bill, mostly to lie back, look at the sky, and think about what you want to think of next.

Take your sabbatical, enjoy the honeymoon. When the enchantment starts to wear off, then begin setting into motion the plans you have made for what you're going to do when you grow up.

Testing New Waters

Bill continued to look forward:

"Maybe I'll decide I want to make more money. That's okay, that would be a conscious decision. I could get more work in my field, I've been getting some calls. But I know I don't want to go back and do what I did. Because I've done it, it was great, and now I don't want the homework anymore. Time to move on to something new.

"Doing some teaching is on my list of possibilities, because I've liked being a mentor, motivating people. I signed up to teach a beginning business class in the community college starting next year, two nights a week. I may be a lousy teacher, I don't know, but I'm going to try it out.

"My wife has always had her own profession. Sometimes she was the corporate wife doing a little traveling with me, sometimes I was the corporate husband going to her things. We've had a fantastic marriage, fantastic kids, and at the same time we've led very separate lives in some ways. So we've never actually tried to live together as much as we're doing now! That is part of the agenda for the future, playing together!

"As a kid, I was never the guy who'd climb up a roof so I could jump off. In my career, though, looking back, I took a lot of risks, although they didn't feel risky at the time — and I know why. It's because I'm a good information gatherer. I like data. I find out what I need to know, I get input from all kinds of sources, maybe I test out an idea or two, and then I'm ready to go.

"So I'm going to take that same approach I've always used regarding what I do next. Experiment a little. Take a course or two. Talk to people. Find out what's really out there."

He had some good strategies. Anticipating the end of the honeymoon, Bill pictured his next moves — and some of those moves, in essence, had a lot to do with learning, thinking, and being like a child:

Look ahead, not back.
Be curious.
Gather information.
Find people to play with.
Find people to help you.
Experiment.
Take chances.
Make mistakes.
Proceed by trial and error, without worrying a whole
    lot about consequences and risks.

How children learn is, in fact, how we all learn and keep moving forward. But we tend to find embarrassing or unacceptable and to stifle some of those tactics as we get older. More rigid, more fearful, we are less willing to fall down, literally and figuratively. And yet that is really what learning is about, and here's a factor in your favor: you are at, or coming to, a place in your life where you don't care as much as you once did what other people think. Or you need not care. In this place, you're not particularly interested in making a good impression. That helps.

So much of adulthood — or the second chapter in your autobiography so far — has unavoidably been defined by the need for self-restraint and by the world's expectations. Now you can pursue a notion simply because something about it tickles your fancy.

As you begin testing the waters, do some "childlike" things.

♦ Hunt out new heroes for the new act of your life to come.

Perhaps the people you have most admired over the years were madcaps who threw caution to the wind, or individuals who consistently placed themselves in a position to help others. Try to spend time with some people like that now. Let what they have rub off on you.

Find a role model or mentor to encourage and inform you along a new avenue you think might be intriguing to explore.

When he was about nine or ten, a high school principal remembered, he spent two summers helping a neighbor plant and care for a victory garden. "Strange as it sounds now, maybe, all these years later," he said, "that was one of the most satisfying experiences of my life. I loved getting my hands in the soil, the amazement of pulling a carrot out of the earth."

His life has been "one hundred percent urban" since then, "never even a philodendron in a pot"; starting to think again about the pleasures of the soil, he took note of an extraordinarily lush flower garden planted in the small spaces around a couple of trees on his city block. He inquired about the tender of the flowers, introduced himself to this new neighbor, who turned out to be an enthusiastic teacher, and found his passion: "I started small and tentatively, with African violets. That led me to the American Gloxinia and Gesneriad Society, and some fabulous people. Now I've become the unofficial gardener-in-residence for my building. And my newest toy — an indoor mini-greenhouse. Orchids on my windowsill next year!" He felt, he said, "as if I've been shot through the heart with love of growing flowers!"

◆ Go to the library and give yourself a school-like assignment; select five books about things you have never done or in areas you have never read about before. See what draws you in.

A doctor looking for new ideas spent an hour in her local bookstore one morning, browsing through the popular For Dummies and Idiots guidebooks. She bought six of them. "Vegetable gardening. Creating Web pages. House selling. Chess. Golf. Shakespeare. I knew nothing about any of these subjects. I read them all, and ended up thinking I might enjoy getting into chess sometime," she said. "But if nothing else, this was an interesting exercise in that it showed me my brain was still working and capable of learning new things."

◆ Make a scrapbook.

As a ten-year-old, were you a dinosaur enthusiast who collected articles about your favorite reptiles, or were you crazy about a glamorous movie star whose pictures you lovingly pasted into albums? Do a grown-up equivalent of that now.

Start a clipping folder. If you have always considered yourself a pretty fair country cook, and you're toying with still-vague notions of how you might spin this ability into something bigger and better, cut out stories and articles about wine growers, buffalo ranchers and restauranteurs, recipes and cookbook reviews, anything to do with food. Get new ideas, maybe the names of people to cold-call for more information or to find a mentor.

Better yet, clip any pieces that catch your eye or spark your curiosity, at least one each day; after a couple of months, pull them out and see what they suggest for your still-vague notion. Fertile ideas often arise from disparate sources. And some entirely novel ideas, ones you hadn't conjured up in the course of your autobiographical exploration, may pop out at you.

A bank manager who calls herself "the ultimate couch potato and perfectly happy there" looked over several months' worth of newspaper and magazine articles she'd saved, and was surprised by how many of them concerned outdoor adventures and the people who take them. "I'm somebody who went camping, once, and hated it," she said. "When we travel, the proximity and cleanliness of bathrooms is one of my top priorities." But something about the outdoor exploits and "ultra sports" she'd read about — "superendurance walks through Death Valley, the Everest Marathon, running downhill from the highest starting line in the world, bike racing, rock climbing" — captivated her. "The participants, and they weren't all young by any means, talked about what they were doing in almost mystical terms," she said. "One of them said something like, Once you've done this, nothing in life seems that difficult anymore."

She wondered if she could add some possibilities to the conclusions she had reached about activities that might engage her in the future, none of which had involved physical exertions. "The most physical thing I've done is give birth to two kids," she said, "but I'm intrigued now by the thought of trying something demanding or tough in that way." Running sounded like a good candidate ("starting with some fast walking"), and she set herself a goal: "Clearly, you have to stick with something long enough to get bitten by the bug, and if what Benjamin Franklin supposedly said is true — repeat an activity daily for three weeks and it becomes an ingrained habit — I'm going to give myself a twenty-one-day assignment and see what happens."

A furniture store buyer who'd had a serious interest as a teenager in American military and naval history amassed a folder of pieces on those subjects, with a new twist. "I used to do a lot of reading about that stuff, and I've visited some of the battlefields," he said. "But what occurred to me was how a lot of people have extended what is essentially a passive or scholarly interest into some neat kinds of activities."

He discovered a group of men who reenacted Civil War battles through a historical association, a woman who began researching that war because of her interest in an 1860s quilt and who became a lecturer on the subject, and "something really terrific — a bunch of people trying to put together an aviation museum for some old World War One and World War Two fighter planes, all restored." He felt a surge of enthusiasm, he said; he thought there might be a number of ways to revive an old interest he hadn't done much with in years and turn it into an active hobby.

◆ Spend some laid-back time with a young child you know and like.

Children are masters of observation. They don't miss a trick; they're eager to learn the whats and whys of all that crosses their path. More than that, the way a youngster interprets the world often has about it a touch of magic, which can be both charming and instructive as you're considering some new ventures for yourself.

Frank T., the fifty-year-old father of a twenty-five-year-old son, hadn't spent much time around young children for years, he said, "other than during the family holiday get-togethers, when my sisters' little kids are all running around like crazy." He decided to separate his four nieces and nephews from the pack, one by one, and get to know them over the course of some relaxed, "going where the wind blows us weekends." He described a weekend with four-year-old Christopher:

"So many small things just kind of struck me. We're

waiting for the subway to go downtown, Christopher wants to see if the train is coming, so we hold hands and he looks down the tunnel. 'Is the train coming?' I ask. And he says, 'I don't know, but the tracks are full of light.' As a grown-up, you skip over that part — you don't notice these gleaming tracks in the dark, you just figure head-lights, train coming."

That evening the uncle and the nephew visited a neighbor's family, and the adults and kids sat around a cheery fire in the fireplace, which had an inset glass fire screen covering the front: "Chris says, 'Why is the glass there?' I said, 'What do you think it's there for?' and he considered this and then he said, 'So you can see the fire really good.' It was a sensible answer, I thought."

In the morning, they did a simple jigsaw puzzle, and when it was finished, Christopher wanted to do it again, then again. "First, I wanted to move on," Frank said. "Then I got into the leisurely rhythm of it, just watching his con-centration, his pleasure in doing it over."

He remembered something that weekend about the process of learning, Frank said, "that it comes in baby steps. . . . Hanging around with a little kid for a while, you realize there's more than one way to see a thing, and sometimes it might be refreshing to turn it on end, come at it from another angle. Also, it can be great to do some-thing over and over, just have fun with it, not rush on to the next something."

Children encourage us to open our eyes again, be ob-servant and curious in ways we perhaps haven't been in a long time, and not worry so much. Watch how a young child approaches a computer. She's not nervous, not fearful about losing all her files. She just pushes buttons, and in that way learns what works and what doesn't, and in that way develops self-confidence.

If you have them, grandchildren can be not just a joy but useful companions in this regard. If you don't have them, find a way to be in the delightful company of small children from time to time.

◆ ◆ ◆

As you gather information, experiment, and try things on for size, be conscious of creeping superego, or:

THE SMALL VOICE OF "I REALLY SHOULD . . ."

A publicist in the TV industry fully anticipated that a major commitment of her after-the-job time would involve "finally doing all the reading I should be doing." Since college and graduate school and throughout her working life, Barbara H. had been storing up a library for the day she'd have time to "really educate myself."

After considering her autobiography, and her motivators and activators, Barbara went to her bookshelves and took a long look at what she'd been keeping with that intent in mind: "I pulled down all these titles, hardcovers and paperbacks. *On the Aesthetic Education of Man*, by Friedrich Schiller. *Verdi Librettos,* in new English translations — also with the original Italian, however! Freud's *The Question of Lay Analysis. The Sunset of the Splendid Century,* a biography of somebody named the Duc du Maine. A life of Beethoven — complete and unabridged! And my favorite — *The Eclogues and Georgics of Virgil,* in the original Latin with a verse translation by C. Day Lewis.

"What was all this stuff? Why did I have it? Did I really want to read these books? I didn't."

The books went, and she felt greatly relieved, even liberated. She did enjoy a good read, Barbara said: "British mysteries, semihistorical novels. A dose of Jane Austen every so often, when I'm feeling anxious about life in general. All fiction and all escapist, I suppose. Nothing *educational.* I'm telling myself now there's nothing wrong with that. I am also giving myself permission not to finish a book if it's not one I'm enjoying."

Ed M., a recent retiree, planned to do volunteer work with old people, for a couple of reasons: "I've never done much in the way of good deeds, helping out people who are worse off than I am. And something else — during their last years, I never was as attentive to my parents as I should have been. They weren't in desperate need of anything, but I know they would have liked to hear from me and see me much more often than they did. So I figured working with older people now would be a way of kind of making up for that."

Through a neighborhood center, Ed took charge of a meals delivery program to shut-in and mostly poor elderly people in his community, scheduling other volunteers, and every Saturday bringing box lunches to some of the several dozen individuals registered for the program. After a year he quit. "I hated it," Ed said. "I had no rapport with these people, and I didn't much like being with them. They looked forward to my visits, so I guess I was doing some good. But I always couldn't wait to get out of those cramped apartments. Just as I was always glad to get away from my folks, although of course I loved them."

Such reactions Ed found enormously guilt-producing, until he thought over what he wanted to do when he grew up and came to some new conclusions. "I worked really hard all my life," he said, "sent three kids through college, did all the house and car repairs myself to keep us going and save money. I always admired others who were giving, altruistic sorts — like one of my heroes, a guy who was very involved in Big Brothers and who sort of took me under his wing for a few years when I was a kid. I don't think I'm that kind of guy myself. Still, I don't know that I really owe anybody anything at this point."

Barbara and Ed had been listening to the small voice that says, "I really should . . ." When they were able to turn that one off, and tell themselves instead, "Well, actually, I don't have to at all, so maybe I shouldn't," they felt much better.

Do launch yourself on the serious greatest books program, if you genuinely are, as was said of the late critic and essayist Alfred Kazin, "the reader who honestly believes that the best and deepest of what we are is on the shelf, and that to read across the shelf changes the self, changes you." Don't burden yourself with such a goal if it's motivated not by passion and pleasure but by a sense that it ought to be one you embrace.

Do help the sick and desperate if it feels like a genuine calling, a deeply satisfying effort, or a needed part of your growing up. Don't berate yourself if it turns out to be not one for you.

At the same time, do pay attention to a certain inertia

that may set in once you have launched a few new schemes. The more a particular path beckons, the more you may resist.

THE RESISTANCE FACTOR

Remember those "high investment" activities, the pursuits that may require from you attention over time, obligation, seriousness, commitment? High-investment activities, it's said, give you the biggest bang for your buck in terms of life satisfaction and well-being. These are the pursuits that will promote the wonderful conviction that you are, indeed, doing what you should be doing with the rest of your life. If you have settled now on an endeavor or endeavors that you have always longed for, if you have been bitten by the bug and go to sleep at night eager for the next day to begin, when you can get back to whatever you're up to, carrying through will probably not be your problem.

On the other hand, if you are toying with some high-investment activities that are difficult, risky, perhaps something you have never tried before, all that commitment, discipline, time, sacrifice, and challenge can begin to sound like a lot of work! We'd just as soon not push ourselves to such levels of involvement, not when we don't have to. And not having to is the key distinguishing feature of this period of free choice. Nothing now — no job requirements, family responsibilities — is compelling you to keep on going except internal conviction.

It's human nature to resist — put off, avoid, divert, forget — what is demanding or involves change. We keep up old habits, even ones we might wish to change, because of an instinctual tendency to maintain stability and hold on to the familiar. Perhaps you have some good ideas in mind but start seeing reasons not to pursue them, or some good intentions that just don't seem to be happening. Perhaps you sense in your bones that the honeymoon is lasting too long; what felt comfortable, relaxing, and like a well-deserved break begins to seem unsatisfying, even oppressive. But you're not making the next moves.

Some voices of resistance, what you just might hear yourself saying once you dream of new paths:

◆ "I am going to get started on this, just not right now. Maybe next year."

The "maybe next year" might make sense if your new plans involve items on an outside agenda — you intend to enroll in a course of study that isn't offered now, say. But if no external obstacles are in the way, "maybe next year" is most likely a delaying tactic, perhaps impelled by a dose of sheer panic. Committing to and investing in a new arena can be a scary business. But if you have done your homework, gathered information, found people to help you, and mulled over your roadblocks and strong suits, then trust your judgment and instincts, and jump into the water. It will not get easier the longer you wait.

◆ "If I start this project, there's no way I'd ever be able to finish. If I commit myself to this cause, there's no way I'll make a real difference."

You have a path in mind but find yourself focusing on the forest rather than the trees, and the forest looks impenetrable. Better to think of small steps and small improvements than to allow yourself to become discouraged before you start.

◆ "I'm too old to do this."

Removing yourself from an arena that intrigues you because you think your timing is all wrong may again be a way of resisting the difficult or different. You may be too old to begin training as a gymnast, because the body just won't go there anymore, but in very few of the nonoccupational endeavors of life are there age limitations.

Whatever form your protests take, if you find yourself stuck, make some time to go back and think over past turning points and your list of activators, considering the roadblocks you would do well to work with or around. You may find there are a few clues, helpful strategies to put into effect now that will help you push yourself off the dime.

One more voice of resistance, a powerful one that can so easily creep in once you have begun whatever you decided to do — especially if you've always been one to set goals extremely high:

◆ "I'll never be very good at this."

You made an all-out effort to follow your dream, the satisfactions are nowhere near what you had anticipated, and you're thinking of throwing in the towel.

Try for a second wind. You just might jump-start your enthusiasm by reexamining your notions of accomplishment and what "very good" means to you.

The Second Wind

Bill continued: "All my adult life I postponed a number of satisfactions; I never had the chance to have any great pleasures outside the workplace and the family. I'm thinking now of a few things I used to love. I loved photography. I loved playing the saxophone.

"However, the thought of being a little good at a bunch of things bothers me. It sounds dilettantish. So I may need to do some work at readjusting that idea. I'm wondering what would be rewarding and what would be fun, and are they both the same? And can I get enough reward and fun out of doing something I'm never going to be terrifically good at?"

Another useful strategy. Once you have tested some waters and plowed ahead with a few new activities, how good at them will you have to be? Can you be content with good enough? And will that call for readjustments in your goals?

GOAL SETTING AND THE GOOD-ENOUGH FACTOR

A retired banker who always enjoyed drawing and painting in his youth, and once entertained the notion of studying architecture although he suspected he didn't have the talent for it, took art classes — acrylic painting, pastels, drawing from live models: "I was tremendously interested in just having some fun with it. And I did. I was painting and sketching all the time. My ability improved dramatically for a while, and then it kind of leveled off. I stopped getting very much better. My paintings looked inferior to what I was seeing in the galleries or even from the others in my classes. And I kind of thought, So that's about all there is there. I lost interest."

For a union official, writing had always been the "fantasy objective." Halfway through writing a novel he'd had in the back of his mind for years, he started thinking: "The book would have to get published," he said, "or what would be the point? Maybe it would even have to be a bestseller. There's a significant risk of huge disappointment if I really put my whole heart and soul into writing something and nobody else thought it was any good. Not in the sense of falling on my face and being considered an idiot in public. But just putting a lot into something and having it go nowhere."

The banker stopped painting and sketching. The union leader stopped writing. Each felt he had fallen short at a critical effort, because each held before him a carrot of success — to become endlessly more talented, to achieve the heights of public recognition — that was probably unattainable. Then, after reflecting a bit more on personal motivators and activators, each got a second wind.

On the job each maintained idealized, overinflated goals, and consequently, neither had considered himself particularly "successful." And yet, by almost any recognizable measure — position, income, the respect of colleagues, the opinions of family and friends — both had done extremely well. In retrospect, each man was able finally to appreciate how far he had come, and to say, "Wow! I really achieved a lot."

That's a perspective they began to apply to their new activities. The banker concluded: "At the start, the real objective of my painting was to do something creative, to go back to something I used to enjoy, to find the pleasure in it. There doesn't have to be a finite end to that objective." And the union official set a new, more modest goal for himself: "Finishing this thing I've wanted to write for a long time will be an accomplishment in itself. After that, we'll see."

Here's a fact to chew over: at the job, you had to or have to worry about getting things right; the line between success and failure, or being accomplished and being ineffectual, is clear — if you keep trying and not succeeding, you're out of a job. In your life after the job, that changes. Trying something and getting it wrong — or not quite right — isn't failing to succeed. If the goal is to try, and you do, you have succeeded. For those of us who are blessed or burdened with a strong achievement drive, or a need to strive for high levels of performance, lowering aspirations may not come easily. Give that some thought.

Suppose you, too, decide to take a stab at being the artist you always thought you had in you, and now you buy paints and canvas and get going — and realize that you have no talent and that painting is for you, in fact, an exercise in absolute frustration. Or you try your hand at writing a novel, decide after plugging away at it for some time that your efforts are embarrassingly amateurish, that your prose is more like the Peanuts dog Snoopy's ("It was a dark and stormy night . . .") than like Updike's, and that a novelist you will never be.

That's okay. Trying and discovering that you're not very good at it or that you don't truly enjoy it after all — and that you'll probably be a lot happier if you put that one to bed and go after something else — keeps you moving forward.

On the other hand, encouraging yourself to be pleased with less than outstanding results — as the banker and the union official did — is a tack you might pursue. You just may discover that "good enough" is all you need. A number of the men and women who offered their thoughts and experiences for this book, the ones who had already put themselves through a fair amount of trial and error and trying things on for size, reported the satisfaction to be uncovered in approximations — achieving if not the Great Accomplishment, something close enough.

The would-be great sportsman runs in a class of age-alikes and finishes in the middle. The would-be master chef learns at Peter Kump's School of Culinary Arts how to prepare a fabulous meal and entertains family and friends.

And it's enough.

A Touch of Inspiration

Three weeks into his postretirement sabbatical was also the occasion of Bill T.'s fifty-fifth birthday, and because he was pondering a twenty-year plan for himself, he thought it might be enlightening and perhaps inspiring to see what some people who had already reached the three-quarter-century mark were doing with their days. He started collecting "people stories," he said, "men and women age seventy-five and up, from gabbing with friends, reading papers, magazines, alumni journals, professional newsletters in my field, whatever I come across."

A few of his favorite people stories:

A seventy-eight-year-old former bandleader and record-company sales representative fashions wildly whimsical sculptures out of discarded or found items — bowling balls, door knockers, candlestick holders, odd scraps of metal, the flotsam and jetsam of tag sales, junkyards and garbage dumps. Museum curators and other art specialists are lately finding his creations stellar examples of "outsider" or "visionary" art, to this amateur craftsman's surprise. "I just thought this stuff was something for an old man to do," he was quoted as saying in a feature article about his work, "to keep from going crazy in his idle, forced retirement."

Martin Gardner, the author of more than sixty books and former *Scientific American* columnist, says he's always hated going to parties or giving speeches, never watches football or basketball or plays golf. What he loves is researching, "learning something new and significant," and writing, which he was still doing at eighty-three. "As my wife long ago realized, I really don't do any *work*," Gardner said in a magazine profile. "I just *play* all the time, and am fortunate enough to get paid for it." Recently he updated an old math book, and it was wonderful, he said, "to learn, for the first time, some basic calculus, and to appreciate fully its enormous elegance and power." And then, "my next greatest pleasure is learning a newly invented magic trick. Conjuring has been a hobby since I was a boy."[17]

A hospital X-ray technician who married at age twenty, had three children by age twenty-six, and retired from her job at seventy, looks back with satisfaction now, at seventy-five, at all she managed to accomplish and would change only one thing: "If I did it all over again, I'd choose to be *only* an independent career woman until I was thirty-five, then I'd start with the family and all the rest of it!" She began thinking about her life after the job about ten years before the fact — reading books about getting older and staying younger, talking to people, checking out some possibilities, making lists. Currently, she said, "I make lunches at a soup kitchen once a week, help out in library bookselling drives twice a year, go to an Elderhostel once a year. I play mahjongg, swim, do aquasize, see my family as often as I can without taking too much of their space, knit, read, nap, and keep in touch with some friends who go back fifty years. I make time for simple joys like playing with the grandchildren and gardening, and I'm always looking around, seeing whatever new situation feels interesting." In her long life, she said, she's been most comfortable with herself "right now. I like my pace and my priorities."

At age eighty, a former advertising executive swims twenty-five-yard laps in the YMCA pool in his community, seventy-five of them at a time, five days a week. He used to swim in college, kept it up sporadically while starting a business and raising a family, coached kids during the summers, then got really serious in the water again when he was in his mid-sixties. Since beginning participation in the United States Masters Swimming program, now competing in the eighty-to-eighty-four age group, he's collected several dozen gold medals and has won national championships. No reason he can't keep competing, he thinks: "I look at my contemporaries. Many have trouble getting up in the morning. They look at themselves as old."

Bill's favorite story came from closer to home: "My father has spent almost all his life in Ohio where we kids grew up, working his parents' farm, later setting up his own small business in real estate and selling insurance. He's ninety now and still working, dealing with a few long-term clients. He's got a tiny office a few minutes away from the house, and he goes home several times a day — home for coffee in the morning with my mother, back to the office, then home for lunch, home for his afternoon coffee. So he's putting in maybe three- or four-hour days, but still at the job, which is the way he wants it."

But Bill's father has other interests, too. "He loves gadgets; he calls himself 'a tinkerer,'" Bill said. "He wanted to be a mechanical engineer and had two years of college before the Depression sent him back to the farm, but all his life he's had his basement workshop — his laboratory, he calls it, putting the emphasis on the second syllable for a joke. He could repair anything. Nobody ever got rid of a vacuum cleaner or a TV or a phonograph that wasn't working; they'd bring it to Pop to fix."

During his honeymoon/sabbatical, Bill went home for a visit and spent several afternoons with his father in the laboratory: "Piles of wires, circuit boards, tools all over. He was dismantling an old oscilloscope someone gave him, just to admire the innards. And he had just finished constructing for himself — or 'fabricating,' as he puts it — a digital clock. This looked like a Rube Goldberg contraption, about two feet tall and a foot wide, not an aesthetically pleasing piece of work but functioning perfectly.

"I told him he could buy a really nifty little digital clock. He looked at me, and he said, 'Where's the fun in that?'"

❖ ❖ ❖

As you write the best story for the rest of your life, designing days that keep you growing and infuse you with an excellent sense of well-being, never forget to look for the fun in it all.

AFTERWORD

ne more story to ponder:
When John and Olivia W. turned fifty-four, both in the same year, they left the world of work — he sold his small manufacturing company, she stopped being a librarian — and had already figured out what they wanted to do next. "We'd planned for a long time to spend a couple of years traveling off and on, do a kind of middle-aged version of the Grand Tour," said Olivia. "Then, John wanted to study Spanish seriously and get into local politics, and I wanted to paint and throw pots."

Three years later, the vision changed: "He knew Spanish; I'd made a lot of pots. We were both getting restless. It was time for something else." He thought he'd like to get his feet back in the business world, she thought she'd like to sell houses. John drummed up a lot of consulting work, Olivia studied for a real estate license and set up a home office.

Some time later still: "Our 'aged p's,' as Dickens called the old folks, dominated the picture for a while," John said. Olivia's parents, both in their early nineties, died within a month of each other, and Olivia spent the better part of a year dismantling the home they had lived in for more than fifty years and settling their complicated estate. Her efforts — distributing family items among her own two children and several nieces and nephews, for one thing — led to frictions with her sisters, which took more efforts to overcome and heal. They also led her "to think I've had enough to do with houses and relatives for a while."

John's parents, during the same period, both needed his attention. "I became caregiver to my mom and dad, absolutely the most difficult role I've ever had," said John, an only child. "Because of my total lack of training and experience, being my parents' keeper was the hardest job I've ever been given in my life." When one of his parents developed Alzheimer's, John became involved in the local Alzheimer's Foundation, and spent much time investigating the research on the disease and doing some fund-raising for the organization.

John and Olivia came out of those experiences in different places. "With me, two sort of surprising things developed," he said. "I became very attached to my Irishness, for the first time. Both my parents were born in Ireland, and I wanted to see what that country might mean to me now, and maybe how I could contribute something there. The second thing was, our friends became a lot more important to me. I felt a need to deepen those ties all of a sudden, maybe because of becoming a middle-aged orphan! Our kids were on their own; the family was so diminished now."

Olivia was less interested in the past than she had ever been. Entertaining and socializing, which John now was loving, was not terribly satisfying to her. "I felt we had a perfect opportunity then to pull up stakes and do something very different," she said. "I read an interview with an English actress, in her sixties, who had sold her house and lived with friends or in sublets when she wasn't on the road. She said she had stopped thinking of herself as 'a person who lives in a certain place,' and she felt so free. I remember being elated by that idea." Olivia saw herself living somewhere, with John, "very simply, a minimalist kind of scene — after our maximalist past lives! I thought I'd be happy at this point being something of an artsy bohemian!"

They had a number of "real, serious, come-to-Jesus discussions about all this," John said. "I was in a mood to hunker down and she was in a mood to fly away." Out of those discussions, they came up with a few plans and compromises — she decided to go back to school to study art history, for one — and a couple of possibilities that would be put on a "future, indefinite" list. Among their deepest and currently somewhat neglected needs, they realized, was to maintain their closeness as a couple, and they decided to develop two new joint interests, ballroom dancing and bridge. "Something neither of us knew anything about," he said, "something we could take lessons in, and do together and with other people."

Said Olivia: "It seems about once every three or four years, like clockwork, we feel compelled to reinvent ourselves."

◆ ◆ ◆

The point of their story: previously defined visions can fade in importance over time. Life keeps happening, and transitions are part of it. You will almost surely confront a few new transitions in the future. (Your partner, simultaneously, may be facing some entirely different ones of his or her own; two individuals are not always changing in tandem.) Perhaps none will be as dramatic as the move from work to nonwork; perhaps some will come down on you like a ton of bricks.

So I would like to leave you with one final suggestion: Put *What Do You Want to Do When You Grow Up?* and your notebook up on the shelf, from whence you might pull them down a year or two or ten in the future for another look. Ideally, you finished your autobiography so far with some new ways of observing yourself, and you translated that into a game plan, a set of actions that will pay off in terms of your well-being when you are no longer spending most of your time at work. Those actions may be exactly right for now, and not so right somewhere down the road.

What I have been outlining here is a process (one that didn't end with the last page), a way to keep thinking about, refining, and experimenting with the rest of your life. It includes a set of tools, skills, and strategies that you may continue to find useful. Review them again at that future juncture, just to see where you are and whether what you're currently doing suits you best.

You may discover at a point of transition that the relative strength and importance of some of your old motivators has shifted, as circumstances change around you and forces change within you. And certain of your old activator roadblocks are no longer in your way, since you have been drawing up a game plan, making choices, and piecing together a vibrant life after the job.

And you just might surprise yourself by finding appropriate and satisfying a completely new set of activities and directions. Which is all to the good, because an iron-clad commitment to one course of action can mean missed opportunities. Growing up always involves a bit of improvisation, shaping and reshaping a life as you go along, and the willingness to refocus and redefine wants and needs.

Perhaps you will decide it's time to move on once again. After all, growing up is never done.

NOTES

Chapter 1

1. M. A. French, "The Windfall of Longevity," Wellesley Centers for Women *Research Report* 2, no. 2 (1999), pp. 4–5.

Chapter 3

2. Erik H. Erikson, *Identity and the Life Cycle* (New York: W. W. Norton & Co., 1980), p. 129.

3. Carol D. Ryff, "Psychological Well-Being in Adult Life," *Current Directions in Psychological Science* 4, no. 4 (1995), pp. 99–103.

4. Gary T. Reker, Edward J. Peacock, and Paul T. P. Wong, "Meaning and Purpose in Life and Well-Being: A Life-Span Perspective," *Journal of Gerontology* 42, no. 1 (1987), pp. 44–49.

5. David J. Ekerdt, Raymond Bosse, and Sue Levkoff, "An Empirical Test for Phases of Retirement: Findings from the Nor-

mative Aging Study," *Journal of Gerontology* 40, no. 1 (1985), pp. 95–101.

6. C. Maslach and J. Goldberg, "Prevention of Burnout: New Perspectives," *Applied and Preventive Psychology* 7 (1998), pp. 63–74.

7. "Leisure," in *Ready or Not,* 20th ed. (New York: Manpower Education Institute, 1993), p. 72.

8. R. A. Stebbins, *Amateurs, Professionals, and Serious Leisure* (Montreal: McGill-Queen's University Press, 1992), as quoted in "High Investment Activity and Life Satisfaction among Older Adults: Committed, Serious Leisure and Flow Activities," by Roger C. Mannell, in *Activity and Aging: Staying Involved in Later Life,* edited by John Robert Kelly (Thousand Oaks, Calif.: Sage Publications, 1993), p. 130.

9. A. R. Herzog, H. Markus, M. Franks, and D. Holmberg, "Activities and Well-Being in Older Age," *Psychology and Aging* 13, no. 2 (1998), pp. 179–85.

Chapter 4

10. Gary Larson, as quoted in "An Amateur of Biology Returns to His Easel," by Natalie Angier, *New York Times,* April 28, 1998, p. F5.

Chapter 5

11. David A. Karp and William C. Yoels, "Work, Careers, and Aging," in *Growing Old in America: New Perspectives on Old Age,* 3d ed., edited by Beth B. Hess and Elizabeth Markson (New Brunswick, N.J.: Transaction Books, 1985), pp. 275–92.

12. Priscilla Roberts and Peter M. Newton, "Levinsonian Studies of Women's Adult Development," *Psychology and Aging* 2, no. 2 (1987), pp. 154–63.

Chapter 6

13. Erica Goode, "New Study Finds Middle Age Is Prime of Life," *New York Times,* Feb. 16, 1999, p. C1.

14. L. L. Carstensen, D. M. Isaacowitz, and S. T. Charles, "Taking Time Seriously: A Theory of Socioemotional Selectivity," *American Psychologist* 54, no. 3 (1999), pp. 165–81.

Chapter 7

15. Jimmy Carter, *The Virtues of Aging* (New York: Ballantine Books, 1998), pp. 89–90.

16. Bruce D. Rapkin and Karla Fischer, "Framing the Construct of Life Satisfaction in Terms of Older Adults' Personal Goals," *Psychology and Aging* 7, no. 1 (1992), pp. 138–49.

Chapter 8

17. Martin Gardner, quoted in "A Mind at Play: An Interview with Martin Gardner," by Kendrick Frazier, *Skeptical Inquirer,* March/April 1998, p. 34–39.

INDEX